RIEL

and the Rebellion 1885 Reconsidered

Thomas Flanagan

Western Producer Prairie Books
Saskatoon, Saskatchewan

Printed and bound in Canada by
Modern Press
Saskatoon, Saskatchewan

Cover design by John Luckhurst

Western Producer Prairie Book publications are produced and
manufactured in the middle of western Canada by a unique publishing
venture owned by a group of prairie farmers who are members of
Saskatchewan Wheat Pool. From the first book published in 1954, a reprint
of a serial originally carried in the weekly newspaper, *The Western Producer*,
to the book before you now, the tradition of providing enjoyable and
informative reading for all Canadians is continued.

Canadian Cataloguing in Publication Data

Flanagan, Thomas, 1944-
    Riel and the Rebellion

Includes index.
ISBN 0-88833-108-8 (bound). — ISBN 0-88833-110-X (pbk.)

1. Riel, Louis, 1844-1885.   2. Riel Rebellion, 1885.
I. Title.
FC3217.R53F53 1983   971.05′4′0924   C83-091372-6
F1060.9.R53F58 1983

CONTENTS

PREFACE

As long as there is a Canada, its citizens will want to read about
Louis Riel because his life summarizes in a unique way the tensions of
being Canadian: English vs. French, native vs. white, East vs. West,
Canadian vs. American. Since I have already written a good deal about
Riel, I would like to clarify the relation of this book to my earlier
writings, for the observant reader may detect some changes in attitude
and tone.

I first became interested in Riel around 1971 when I conceived the
idea of writing an account of his prophetic religious mission from the
inside, as it were — as he understood himself, not as others had
labeled him, a victim of mental disease. While I worked on that
interpretation, I edited some of Riel's writings for publication, chiefly
his diaries and the poetry of his youthful years in Montreal.[1] My
biographical treatment of Riel appeared in 1979 under the title *Louis
"David" Riel: "Prophet of the New World."*[2] Perhaps I should have
stopped there, but Riel still continued to fascinate me. Therefore I
agreed to participate in the Louis Riel Project, headed by the historian
G. F. G. Stanley, which was organized to edit all of Riel's writings for
publication in 1985, the centennial year of the North-West Rebellion.[3]
My particular assignment was to edit the volume containing
everything authored by Riel between 4 June 1884, when he was
invited to involve himself in the politics of the Saskatchewan District,
and 16 November 1885, when he was hanged for his role in the
North-West Rebellion. Since my volume was in essence a documen-
tary history of the Rebellion, I had to make a more careful study than I
had done before of the events and issues of that movement. Previously
interested in Riel as a religious figure, I had taken my guidance on

political questions more or less uncritically from what earlier historians had written. But as I went over the story again and made my own study of the primary sources, the conventional account began to seem inadequate. I had accepted that the *Métis* had serious unresolved grievances; that the government of Canada never gave a satisfactory response to their complaints; that Riel resorted to violence only after legal means of action had failed; that he received a trial of questionable validity before being executed by a vengeful government. As I sifted the evidence, this view became less and less convincing to me, until I concluded that the opposite was closer to the truth: that the *Métis* grievances were at least partly of their own making; that the government was on the verge of resolving them when the Rebellion broke out; that Riel's resort to arms could not be explained by the failure of constitutional agitation; and that he received a surprisingly fair trial. When I came to these conclusions, I knew I had to publish them, especially because of the gathering movement to grant Riel a posthumous pardon in 1985, something which now strikes me as quite wrong. I might have written my version of events as an introduction to my volume of the Riel Papers; but the Social Sciences and Humanities Research Council of Canada, which has so generously funded the Riel Project, wished such introductions to be kept short. Thus what might have been an introduction to a very large book has become a small book in its own right.

Let me make a few comments about terminology. Traditionally in Canadian historiography, the events of 1869-70 were known as the Red River Rebellion and those of 1885 as the North-West Rebellion. The late W. L. Morton suggested it would be more appropriate to call the former the "Red River Resistance" on the grounds that formation of a Provisional Government in a situation where no other government existed did not constitute rebellion against the Crown. Like most researchers in the field, I agree and have adopted Morton's terminology. However, I continue to refer to the events of 1885 as the North-West Rebellion. Riel's council bore the strange name of Exovedate, but it was understood to be, and often called by all participants, a provisional government. Riel's followers not only formed a government, they took hostages, demanded to negotiate with Canada, and fought pitched battles with the police and militia. I think "rebellion" is the proper word for what they did.

As all students of North American mixed-blood people know, it is hard to find satisfactory terms to describe them. Conferences on mixed-blood history always produce wrangling over terminology. I have here adopted the following policy. When I refer to people of mixed Indian-white ancestry in the context of twentieth-century Canada, I write "Métis," which I would pronounce [Mā-tee]. When I

refer generally to mixed bloods in the nineteenth century, whether
English or French, I write "half-breed," the prevailing term in the
English language at that time, although I realize the word is today
offensive to many people, especially white liberals who sympathize
with native aspirations. (Interestingly, contemporary Métis spokesmen often are proud to be called half-breed.) However, it was a more
neutral term a century ago, and I hope I will be allowed to use it in that
context. When I refer specifically to the French-speaking half-breeds
in Manitoba or the North-West, I write "*Métis*," italicized to show that
it is a French word and should be pronounced [Mā-tēs]. It is important
to have a precise designation for the French half-breeds, for they
constituted a cohesive social group. They often called themselves "the
new nation," showing consciousness of a distinct identity which did
not include the English half-breeds, whose racial ancestry was equally
mixed but who did not participate in the same community. It was
these *Métis* whom Louis Riel considered his own people and whom he
called *la nation métisse-canadienne-française.*

It is a pleasure at this point to thank the numerous institutions and
individuals without whose help this book could not have been
completed. The research was supported financially by the Louis Riel
Project with money donated by the Social Sciences and Humanities
Research Council of Canada. The University of Calgary also granted
me financial assistance in connection with the Riel Project. The
University of Alberta in sponsoring the Project provided a location
and much technical, administrative, and financial support. I am
grateful to the employees of the various archives whose holdings I
consulted during the research; the institutions are named in the List of
Abbreviations. The prior work of G. F. G. Stanley has been
particularly valuable to me. Although my conclusions are sometimes
different from his, I could never have done my research without his
pioneering efforts to build on. Miriam Carey and Donald Smith gave
me important insights into the collaboration between Riel and
William Henry Jackson. Neil Watson used his expertise in legal
history to help me analyze Riel's trial. *Saskatchewan History* and the
Revue de l'Université d'Ottawa graciously granted me permission to
rework portions of articles previously published in those journals. I
extend my thanks to all these people as well as to many others whose
names are not mentioned here.

CHAPTER ONE

THE NORTH-WEST REBELLION

On a world scale of violence, Canada's North-West Rebellion of 1885 was a trifling affair. Two or three hundred able-bodied *Métis* from the settlements along the South Saskatchewan River took up arms. They were joined at Batoche by an even smaller number of Indians. A few other Indian bands rose in an uncoordinated spasm of murder and pillage — the Crees of the Battle River country and the Assiniboines of the Eagle Hills — but the large majority of Plains Indians, as well as *Métis*, remained out of the conflict, even though they were approached by emissaries from Riel. The Canadian government fielded about 8,000 men, divided into several different columns, plus the usual complement devoted to logistical support. Thus the largest fighting unit, that led by General Middleton against Batoche, numbered less than a thousand men. Other units sent against the Indians were considerably smaller. The number of casualties was correspondingly low. There is some uncertainty about the numbers of *Métis* and Indians who died in the campaign, but it is safe to say that about a hundred men lost their lives in all engagements together.

Of course, these numbers are not the whole story; they must be set in the context of a thinly populated frontier society. If the total of deaths is not impressive, the number of casualties, including wounded, was high compared to the numbers engaged. The fighting covered huge distances and it was expensive. The direct cost of the Rebellion to the Canadian government was over $5,000,000, a substantial sum for the day. More importantly, this was Canada's first independent military venture. General Frederick Middleton and a few other senior officers were British career soldiers; but the fighting men and middle officers were all Canadian, as were the political direction and financial support. The Rebellion proved that Canada could successfully make a major military effort over great reaches of its own territory. It thus occupies a place in Canadian military history more significant than mere statistics might seem to warrant.

However, the true importance of the Rebellion in our history is more symbolic than military. The Rebellion will always be remembered because it expressed several of the fundamental tensions of Canada: the aspirations of western settlers to run their own affairs versus the desire of Ottawa to control the public domain according to its own conception of national interest; the conviction of natives, both Indians and Métis, that this was "their land," versus the belief of white men in British sovereignty; the conflicting sympathies of English and French Canadians toward the French-speaking, Catholic Métis; the desire of some in the West for union with the United States; and the quite realistic fear among Canadian statesmen that annexation would follow if Canada did not show a strong hand on the prairies.

These tensions were all concentrated in the person of Louis Riel, who led the Métis into battle and who was executed as a traitor when his movement failed. He was a human bridge between the poles of these antagonisms. Born and raised in Red River, he had been educated at Montreal; thus he knew both East and West. A Métis of seven-eighths white ancestry, he united Indian and white in his own blood. His mother tongue was French, but he spoke English well. He had modified his ardent Roman Catholicism to the point where he now preached an exotic new religion to which Protestants and Catholics alike were invited to adhere. Born a British subject, he had renounced his allegiance to Queen Victoria and become an American citizen in 1883. Small wonder that his career, and particularly his lonely appearance in the prisoner's box at Regina, has captured the Canadian imagination. He thus symbolizes in one way or another so many of the great issues which have constituted the agenda of our history.

As we approach the centennial of the North-West Rebellion, it is time to have another look at the man and the movement. Myth makers of all kinds have been and will be at work, making Riel into a western separatist, a francophone martyr, a native rights activist, even *mirabile dictu* a Canadian nationalist. Although several good histories of the Rebellion and biographies of Riel have been written, there is still much that is obscure about his role in the Rebellion. The obscurities linger particularly about the most controversial questions. What were the grievances of the Métis? Did the government respond to them? What were Riel's real objectives in 1885? Did he receive a fair trial?

The book is not a broad history of the Rebellion; it is a detailed study of the issues which were at stake.[1] History is not a morality play in which one side represents good and the other evil. Nonetheless, we cannot help making moral judgments about significant past events. We want to know: was Riel, were the *Métis*, justified in resorting to arms? Was the government justified in subjecting Riel to the highest punishment of the law? Should he be pardoned one hundred years later? The research embodied in this book is meant to encourage informed answers to such questions. It will serve its purpose if it raises the level of discussion above slogans and catch-words by showing the true issues in the context of their day. To set the stage for the discussion of particular issues, I here give a brief sketch of events.

All historians agree that the origins of the Rebellion must be traced to the "Resistance" of 1869-70 in the Red River Colony. The *Métis*, led by the young Louis Riel, frustrated the transfer of Rupert's Land from the Hudson's Bay Company to Canada until their demands were met. Thinking to ensure their survival as a distinctive francophone and Catholic community, they insisted on guarantees of their autonomy, such as provincial rather than territorial status, bilingual government institutions, confessional schools, and local control of public lands. These demands were granted in a formal way in the Manitoba Act of 1870, except that a land grant to mixed-blood people was substituted for provincial control of the public domain. However, the outcome was not favorable to the *Métis* in the long run. Their resistance created antipathy among the largely English-speaking Protestant settlers who streamed into the new province of Manitoba. The francophone element was quickly outnumbered and outmaneuvered in local politics. The land grant was slow in implementation; and when it did come, it was designed to facilitate quick sale to land speculators. Before the decade was up, the *Métis*, and indeed many of the English half-breeds, had begun to feel like strangers in their native land. They emigrated by thousands to places farther west: Montana, Cypress Hills, Wood Mountain, Qu'Appelle, and especially the valley of the South Saskatchewan. In the late 1870s and early 1880s, the river banks south of Prince Albert were populated by hundreds of *Métis* and half-breed families spread out somewhat as they had been on the Red River, with the English to the north, the French to the south. The center of *Métis* settlement was the parish of St. Laurent, including the village of Batoche.

Almost from the beginning the *Métis* who settled along the South Saskatchewan began directing complaints to the federal government. Fortunately, documents have survived which record these grievances in their own words. The first statement of *Métis* grievances was a letter from Gabriel Dumont to the lieutenant-governor of the North-West Territories, reporting a meeting held at St. Laurent, 1 February 1878.[2]

The letter requested four things: that the governor appoint a French magistrate and a *Métis* member of the Territorial Council; that the Territorial government subsidize local schools; that there be a land grant, as in Manitoba, to extinguish the aboriginal title of the half-breeds; and that agricultural assistance be offered to the *Métis* farmers of St. Laurent.

From 1882 to 1884 half a dozen more letters and petitions came from St. Laurent to various officials of local and federal government.[3] All dealt solely with the issue which was now paramount at St. Laurent: the application of the homesteading rules of the Department of the Interior to the *Métis* who were settling along the South Saskatchewan River. They wanted a survey or resurvey of the banks into river lots, as well as relaxation of certain rules which interfered with their preferred style of settlement.

A comprehensive list of *Métis* demands was drawn up at the time of the Territorial elections of March 1883. When the two candidates for the district of Lorne came to St. Laurent, they were presented with this fourteen-point list, and both endorsed its contents. The document included concerns which had already been voiced in letters of complaint: more French officials in government; a half-breed land grant in the North-West; easing of homestead regulations and granting of river lots; and continued support of local schools. A number of new requests were also evident. Some were concerns of a local nature that might be voiced by any community, such as improvement of ferries and construction of roads. Others were far-reaching political objectives, such as provincial status for the District of Saskatchewan and representation of the Territories in the House of Commons. It is clear from the context that these items were all goals which the *Métis* desired to attain but did not necessarily consider serious grievances. Louis Schmidt, who reported this list to *Le Manitoba*, commented: "We do not expect all these requests to be granted. We wanted to show that there was still much to be done to satisfy us."[4]

The issues which did produce a deep sense of grievance appeared in a list of seven items produced in the spring of 1884 when the *Métis* of St. Laurent held a series of protest meetings, in some of which English half-breeds from the Prince Albert area participated. This document was taken to Louis Riel by the delegation that was sent to seek his advice in Montana. It is the single best record of *Métis* grievances, that is, of unfulfilled demands in which they discerned injustice.

We, the French and English natives, being convinced that the government of Canada has taken possession of the North-West

Territories without the consent of the natives . . . both the French
and English natives claim as their right:

1) to participate in at least the same rights and privileges
claimed by the [natives] of Manitoba, seeing that the North-
West is much wealthier in resources, etc.

2) that the French and English natives claim the right of being
represented in the North-West council, based on the native
population living here.

3) that the French and English natives of the North-West
(those that have not participated in the Manitoba lands grant)
want free Patent for the lands they possess and occupy at the
present date, without any prejudice to any more grants to which
they are entitled for the extinction of their indian title to the
lands of the North-West.

4) that the natives, French and English, protest against the
dues and charges on Timber and forests until their rights within
mentioned be recognized and granted by the Dominion government.

5) that the management of the Indians' affairs such as Indian
agents, Instructorships or other offices for the benefit of the
Indians in the North West Territories be entrusted to natives, as
they are more familiar with the habits, character and wants of
those Indians, and to prevent any regrettable occurrences as
have happened in the past.

6) that the French and English natives of the North-West
having never recognized any right to the lands of this
North-West assumed by the Hudson's Bay Company or by the
Dominion Government, claim an exclusive right to those lands
along with the Indians.

7) that the French and English natives of the North-West
knowing that Louis Riel has made a bargain with the government of Canada in 1870, which said bargain is contained mostly
in what is known as "the Manitoba Act" and this meeting not
knowing the contents of said "Manitoba Act," we have thought
it advisable that a delegation be sent to said Louis Riel and have
his assistance to bring all the matters referred to in the above
resolutions in a proper shape and form before the government of
Canada, so that our just demands be granted.[5]

This list is remarkable for the extent to which its contents deal with
land. Only two points — better representation in the North-West
council and more government jobs — are unconnected to land. The
rest of the items interlock to form a distinct position, which may be
briefly summarized. The half-breeds are an aboriginal people who,

along with the Indians, were the original owners of Rupert's Land. Their aboriginal title must be extinguished in the North-West, as it was in Manitoba, through a land grant. In the meantime, it is unjust to limit their access to timber resources of which they are still the true owners. Also, as original settlers, they should be allowed free patent for lands they have already occupied. Much the same points were made by Charles Nolin and Maxime Lépine to Bishop Grandin when he visited St. Laurent in June 1884.[6] Thus all evidence points to the land question as being the most fundamental concern of the Métis at the time the delegation was sent to Riel. This was also consistently expressed in the Métis letters to government going back to 1878. Other complaints come and go, but various aspects of the land question appear in every single document produced by the Métis.

When they produced their seven-point list of grievances, the Métis and half-breeds decided to send it to Louis Riel for his advice. Accordingly, they despatched in May 1884, a delegation consisting of three locally important men: Gabriel Dumont, the acknowledged leader of St. Laurent; his brother-in-law Moïse Ouellette, himself the leader of an extensive Métis clan; and James Isbister, the first half-breed to have farmed near the site of Prince Albert. The younger and less influential Michel Dumas accompanied them at his own expense. They arrived on 4 June at St. Peter's mission, Montana, where Riel was teaching school.

Much had happened to Riel since the glory days of 1870 when he had been president of the provisional government at Red River. He had had to flee his homeland to escape the vengeance of Colonel Garnet Wolseley's Ontario volunteers when the Expeditionary Force arrived in August 1870. For three years he had shuttled back and forth between Minnesota and Manitoba, waiting in vain to receive a pardon for the misguided execution of Thomas Scott, which he had sanctioned in his days of power. Then in 1873 he went east, to press his own case as Member of Parliament for the riding of Provencher. Eighteen months of intense politicking finally produced a conditional amnesty: Riel would be pardoned for the Scott affair, but only if he left Canada for five years. He was also deprived of his seat in the House of Commons. This new setback accelerated Riel's growing sense of religious mission. He believed God was subjecting him to these trials only to prepare him for a greater glory yet to come. On 8 December 1875 Riel experienced a spiritual breakthrough while attending mass in Washington, D.C. He became convinced that the Holy Spirit was speaking to him and through him to the world at large; he was now the "Prophet of the New World."

His friends interpreted this prophetic exaltation as the onset of madness and placed him in insane asylums in the province of Quebec for almost two years. While thus confined, he wrote at length about the new dispensation of which he was the prophet. The *Métis* would be the second Chosen People who would purify Catholicism by reviving many of the practices of the Hebrews, the first Chosen People. The Holy Spirit would leave the corrupt Roman papacy to settle upon Riel's patron Ignace Bourget, Bishop of Montreal. When Riel was discharged from Beauport asylum in January 1878, he had learned to keep his revelations to himself, but he continued to believe in them with undiminished fervor.

After some half-hearted attempts to settle in New York, Riel went to the American West. When he failed to interest Bishop John Ireland of St. Paul, Minnesota, in a colonization scheme for French Canadians from New England, he pushed on to Montana, where numerous *Métis* and Indians had congregated to follow the last buffalo herd in North America. Riel tried to organize them for an invasion of Canada in the spring of 1880, but that plan also failed. He then supported himself for a few years as a petty trader, taking goods on consignment and selling them to *Métis* and Indians for buffalo robes. He involved himself in Montana politics on the side of the Republicans and became episodically notorious in the local press when he was accused of illegally inducing British half-breeds to vote in the election of November 1882. Along the way he married Marguerite Monet *dite* Bellehumeur, the daughter of a *Métis* hunter, and became the father of two children. He settled at the Jesuit mission of St. Peter's, on the Sun River between Helena and Fort Benton, in the spring of 1883, and prepared to earn a meager living as a school teacher. Externally normal in behavior and orthodox in religion, he still clung to his belief that he was a divinely inspired prophet. His mission was alive but dormant, waiting for a signal from God in order to become public once again. His private papers show that he went through an intense spiritual crisis in the spring of 1884, immediately before the arrival of the delegation from the Saskatchewan District. When they reached him, he was ready for a challenge.

The delegation had been instructed to present several options to Riel. He could remain in Montana and advise the Saskatchewan Valley settlers from afar; he could travel to Ottawa to present their case to the federal government; or he could come to St. Laurent to participate in the movement directly. With little hesitation, Riel chose the third alternative. His letter of acceptance made plain that he was coming not only to help his fellow countrymen but to press certain claims of his own for financial compensation from the government.

After Riel arrived in St. Laurent in early July, there ensued a lengthy period of peaceful political agitation. Working closely with William Henry Jackson, a young Liberal from Prince Albert, Riel tried to frame a petition of grievances which would be acceptable to all residents of the area, native as well as white, anglophone as well as francophone. This was no simple task; for while all parties had many complaints for which they held Ottawa to blame, they also differed among themselves over the preeminent question of native land rights. The petition sent to Ottawa, 16 December 1884, emphasized the concerns of the white settlers of Prince Albert more than those of the *Métis*, but it also hinted at more radical demands to follow.

The government by now was becoming worried about events in the West. On 28 January 1885, the cabinet authorized an enumeration of the half-breed population of the North-West Territories in preparation for a land grant similar to that which had been given in Manitoba. About the same time the Department of the Interior reached a resolution of the river-lot question which had vexed the St. Laurent colony for so long. But these concessions, communicated to the *Métis* in February and March, did not cause the agitation to subside. If Riel had ever been much interested in these petty matters, he had now gone far beyond them. He was emphasizing that the *Métis* and half-breeds were the true owners of the North-West and that their claims must be satisfied by creation of a vast trust fund for future generations. Also, the voice of the Holy Spirit was becoming ever more peremptory, telling him the time for public revelation was near. These radical impulses were strengthened by his disappointment with the government for not recognizing his personal claims for money. He had entered into behind-the-scenes negotiations in December and January to try to secure a sum of money from the prime minister, but these had proven fruitless.

These motives are clear enough, but their precise operation in Riel's mind may remain obscure forever, unless new documentation for the first three months of 1885 is discovered. In any case, he took up arms with the *Métis* on 18 March. They remained almost alone in this desperate enterprise as their former partners in the movement, the English half-breeds and white settlers, refused to support them. Only a few Indians from neighboring reserves joined in, while the Crees of the Battle River and the Assiniboines of the Eagle Hills, excited by the rising, went on separate ventures of pillage and destruction. For a week the *Métis* were guilty only of taking hostages, cutting telegraph lines, and looting stores; but they crossed the line of open rebellion when they fought a pitched battle against the North-West Mounted Police at Duck Lake, 26 March. That pyrrhic victory ensured that Riel's stated objective of entering into negotiation with the government could not be achieved, for Canada would have to recover its prestige with force.

Failing to secure widespread support, the *Métis* waited at Batoche for the inevitable attack. While digging trenches for military defense, they were also occupied with Riel's religious reforms. He openly emerged in his role of prophet, announcing that Rome had fallen and that Bishop Bourget was now pope. The Lord's Day was changed from Sunday to Saturday, and Riel organized religious services while the missionaries were put under house arrest. As the Métis council, dubbed by Riel the Exovedate (from the Latin words *ex* "from" and *ovile* "flock"), debated these matters, the Canadian forces drew nearer. The Métis temporarily checked their advance with an ambush at Fish Creek 24 April, but the final battle could only be postponed, not avoided. Batoche fell after four days of fighting, 9 May to 12 May. Meanwhile separate columns dealt with the Indians.

Events now shifted from the military to the legal plane. Even though he probably could have escaped to Montana, Riel voluntarily surrendered to General Middleton. He unrealistically hoped to have a great trial before the Supreme Court of Canada to publicize his cause to the world. Instead he was taken to Regina to be tried for high treason before a stipendiary magistrate. After four days of oral argument, he was convicted on 1 August and received the mandatory death sentence. Execution was postponed while unsuccessful appeals were made to the Manitoba Court of Queen's Bench and the Judicial Committee of the Privy Council. There was also a further short delay while a medical commission appointed by the cabinet verified Riel's sanity. He was finally hanged on 16 November.

Most other participants in the Rebellion were treated with relative leniency. Only eighty-five persons were tried for any crime; all others were allowed to go back to their farms or reserves without legal penalty. Apart from Riel, the only men to be hanged were eight Indians shown to have murdered unresisting victims. Most Indians and Métis received sentences of seven years or less for treason-felony and were paroled after serving about a year. The government's strategy was clearly to make Riel the symbol of the Rebellion and punish him accordingly. This served the government's purpose in the short run but has had the long-term effect of making Riel a mythical figure. He went to the scaffold believing that, like Christ, he would rise from the dead on the third day. That did not happen, but his death has given him a different form of immortality in the collective Canadian self-consciousness.

As the Rebellion's centennial approaches, our attention keeps coming back to Riel. What do we make of his role in the Rebellion? This is not a new concern; in fact, the main answers to the question were all represented at the trial in the views of the prosecution, of Riel himself, and of his defense attorneys.

The prosecution held that the Rebellion was wholly unjustified.

The minor grievances of the *Métis* certainly were not enough to require an armed uprising against the state, and in any case the government was already moving to respond to their complaints. The alleged grievances were only pretexts for Riel to provoke an uprising in furtherance of his private interests. This account was consistently maintained by the prime minister and other government spokesmen in the polemics of the day. It was also current in the English-language books published in the last century about the North-West, but it is hardly represented today in the historical literature. Its only proponent in recent decades is Donald Creighton, whose biography of Sir John A. Macdonald gave the governmental interpretation of the Rebellion.[7]

Riel's own position was exactly the opposite. He maintained that the Rebellion was a wholly justified response to oppression. The *Métis* had serious grievances which had never been remedied. They took up arms only in self-defense when the government threatened to attack them with a column of Mounted Police. Riel claimed that he had never acted except from disinterested motives. This interpretation was shared by Gabriel Dumont[8] and many other *Métis*, past and present. It was advanced in A.-H. de Trémaudan's *Histoire de la nation métisse dans l'Ouest Canadien*, which was published posthumously by the Union Nationale Métisse Saint Joseph du Manitoba.[9] More recently, it was revived by Howard Adams, who embroidered Trémaudan's account with speculations that the Rebellion was provoked by a government *agent provocateur* in an attempt to discredit Riel and the *Métis*.[10]

The third view, that of Riel's defense attorney, is more complicated than the first two. His counsel argued that the *Métis* had important complaints which had been shamefully neglected by the government. While these did not perhaps justify an insurrection, they were certainly mitigating circumstances. But the Rebellion itself was a product of Riel's insanity. The credulous *Métis* had been led by a madman who should not be convicted because he was not capable of criminal intent. The peculiar attraction of this interpretation is that it offers middle ground between the uncompromising postures of Riel and the prosecution. One does not have to support the Rebellion, but one can still criticize the government on two counts: causing the violence by inaction and hanging a madman.

In 1885, this view was taken by most of the Liberal opposition, by French ecclesiastics such as Archbishop Taché, and by the many French Canadians who were opposed to Riel's execution. Like the prosecution's theory, it quickly found its way into the historical literature; but while the former has lost favor and almost disappeared, the latter has steadily won adherents and now dominates the field. The turning point was probably George Stanley's pioneering study,

The Birth of Western Canada (1936). Stanley devoted a whole chapter to the *Métis* grievances and strongly supported their case: "The justice of the *Métis* case cannot but be admitted. . . . The case against the Government is conclusive . . . constitutional agitation *and* the petition had been an acknowledged failure." The Rebellion itself "was the scheme of a madman, but Riel was no longer sane."[11]

All subsequent historians of the Rebellion and biographers of Riel have drawn on Stanley's version of history.[12] Its appeal has been strengthened by the judgment of numerous psychiatrists who have written papers to prove that Riel was mentally ill.[13] It was also maintained by Stanley himself in his later book *Louis Riel* (1963), although the attentive reader will notice that the author's views have become less pronounced.[14] Nowhere does the book definitely state that Riel was insane in 1885, and material is presented which casts doubt on the validity of the *Métis* grievances. But the increasing ambivalence of Stanley's position has not had as much influence on general opinions as the clear-cut pronouncements of his early work. Of recent writers, only Desmond Morton has challenged the reigning orthodoxy, and that only in passing.[15]

These trends in the academic literature have helped rehabilitate Riel's popular reputation, so that he now appears more a hero and victim than a traitor and criminal. The effect has been powerfully reinforced by wider trends in public opinion. Following World War II, those parts of the world which once belonged to European empires have gained their political independence. "National liberation" is now a sacred invocation at the United Nations. Increasingly, native leaders in North America have come to identify their aspirations with those of the Third World, as in George Manuel's concept of the "Fourth World."[16] Indians and other aboriginal peoples who constitute internal minorities within nations dominated by men of European ancestry are the "Fourth World," who are fighting the same struggle for emancipation that has been successfully concluded in the Third World. Riel now appears to many as Canada's own leader of national liberation, a home-grown Fidel Castro or Ho Chi Minh.

Perhaps not everyone sees Riel in quite this light, but many conversations have convinced me there is now a wide popular consensus on several points: that the *Métis* were badly treated by Canada, that Riel was a well-meaning idealist motivated by concern for the welfare of his people, and that his trial in 1885 was very unfair. Not surprisingly, it has now been suggested several times that it would be appropriate to grant Riel a posthumous pardon in connection with the centennial of the Rebellion which will take place in 1985. The Association of Métis and Non-Status Indians of Saskatchewan has formally proposed this to the federal cabinet,[17] and the idea keeps popping up on the floor of Parliament as well as in the press.

Now is therefore a good time to review Riel's role in the Rebellion. Important new sources of information have become available since George Stanley's authoritative biography of Riel was published in 1963. The researcher can now have access to the files of the Department of the Interior, which contain much information about the grievances of the *Métis*. The Louis Riel Project has collected all of Riel's papers whose whereabouts are known.[18] Also, there have been many studies of Riel and the *Métis* which sometimes put old and familiar facts in a new light.[19]

This book will focus on those questions which are most relevant to making overall moral judgments about Riel and the Rebellion. Since the two are now such an integral part of our collective self-consciousness, we cannot avoid making evaluations of them. We want to be able to say, in some broad sort of way, whether the Rebellion was indeed justified and Riel was thus a martyr, or whether it was a needless act of violence and Riel got what he deserved, a traitor's death. The old questions — rebel or hero, traitor or martyr? — will not go away, even when they become clichés, because they are the ultimately important questions for an evaluation of our national history. Did Canada disgrace itself in its handling of the Rebellion, or did it respond with appropriate firmness to an unacceptable challenge to public authority?

The following questions are discussed, each in its own chapter:

1. What were the difficulties of the *Métis* concerning river lots and how did the government react to their complaints?
2. Did the *Métis* and half-breeds of the North-West have a right to a land grant as in Manitoba? Again, what did the government do about it?
3. What was Riel's real object in the agitation? Upon what principle did he base the demands of the *Métis*?
4. To what extent, if any, was Riel influenced by narrow considerations of personal financial gain?
5. Did he receive a fair trial?
6. Should his sentence have been commuted because of his alleged insanity?
7. In light of answers to the first six questions, is there a good argument for granting Riel a posthumous pardon?

These questions are inherently controversial. Even exhaustive study of all the facts may leave reasonable men holding opposite views. But if factual knowledge is not sufficient to resolve all disagreements, it will surely help bring the debates into sharper focus.

I hope the primary contribution of this book will be to set these questions in the context of the day, so that we can see them with historical appreciation for the dilemmas they embody. Some readers may disagree with my conclusions because they attribute more or less weight to certain factors, but they will have to take account of the evidence assembled here before their opinions can be persuasive.

CHAPTER TWO

RIVER LOTS AND LAND CLAIMS

There were many *Métis* living in 1870 in those parts of Rupert's Land which, upon acquisition by Canada, would become the North-West Territories. With a few exceptions, the major one being the settled community of St. Albert, these *Métis* were traders and buffalo hunters who did not have well-established claims to particular pieces of land. They often had cabins in several widely scattered locations which they might use for wintering, but they did not typically have farms on which they permanently resided. In the 1870s, as the buffalo grew less numerous and finally vanished, the *Métis* of the North-West began to settle down, invariably staking out long, narrow lots for themselves along river banks. They were reinforced in this pattern of land holding by the thousands of *Métis* who emigrated from Manitoba in this period. Already accustomed to having such lots along the Red and Assiniboine rivers, they naturally followed the same pattern when they settled on the Saskatchewan.

This preference for river lots embroiled the *Métis* in difficult disputes with the Department of the Interior, which was committed to surveying the North-West Territories on the rectangular plan. The resulting conflicts are often cited as a major cause of the Rebellion, with the implication that bureaucratic single-mindedness threatened to dispossess the *Métis* of the claims they had staked in good faith.

The issue is a tangled one which can only be understood through painstaking, detailed study. Upon this type of scrutiny, stereotypes and exaggerated claims dissolve. It quickly becomes apparent that the *Métis* and the Department of the Interior were not totally at odds. The department allowed river lots to be obtained under certain circumstances, and the *Métis* generally admitted the right of the department to set up regulations for ownership and registration of land. The actual disputes were technical in nature: What were the rights of those who had settled before survey as compared to those who had settled afterwards? Would land surveyed on the rectangular plan be resurveyed into river lots? How would river lots be legally described and recorded? Under which version of homesteading rules, which naturally underwent amendment over time, would *Métis* claims be adjudicated?

Analysis at this level shows that the rights and wrongs of the controversy are to be found on both sides. Government employees made obvious mistakes in judgment, and the Department of the Interior had special problems of dishonesty and inefficiency in this period. The *Métis*, badly advised by their missionary priests, were unrealistic in their expectations and sometimes deliberately flouted regulations when they could have conformed without hardship. Both government officials and *Métis* settlers consistently misperceived the difficulties under which the other labored. It was, in short, like most problems in human relations, a train of mistakes, misjudgments, and misperceptions on both sides. But in the end a reasonable compromise was proposed and executed by the Department of the Interior. Tragically, the *Métis* at this point were unwilling to accept the compromise, so that it did not prevent an insurrection. The river-lot question was a cause of the Rebellion in the subjective sense that it helped create the acrimony which led to the rising; but it was not a cause in the objective sense that the *Métis* had no way other than violence to get the kind of land holdings they desired. As far as river lots are concerned, it was a story of missed opportunities for reconciliation rather than one of rebellion provoked by unrelenting oppression.

DOMINION LANDS

The land claims of the *Métis* cannot be understood without knowing something about the administration of Dominion Lands. This information would have been commonplace in an earlier era, but today's reader may appreciate a brief review of the subject.[1]

The government of Canada was determined from the first to retain control of the lands obtained by the purchase of Rupert's Land from the Hudson's Bay Company. This was imperative if the government was to guide immigration, settlement, and railway construction for national ends. One consequence of this policy was uniformity of administration of Dominion Lands from the Red River to the Rockies. It was decided to survey and subdivide this immense territory as an integral whole. A survey system closely modeled on the American one was adopted in 1871, but it was to be applied in a better way. The

American public domain was surveyed at many different times, from various starting points, and often in great haste with inaccurate results. Settlement raced ahead of survey, leaving painful adjustments to be made later. Canada proposed to survey the arable part of the West in one process, from one starting point, working methodically and carefully before settlers arrived to complicate things.

These aims were largely achieved. The first step, taken in 1871, was to establish the Winnipeg Meridian (approximately 102° West of Greenwich). This, in conjunction with the forty-ninth parallel, served as a starting point for the survey of Manitoba and adjacent parts of the Territories. Three years of work subdivided enough land to provide for settlement in the foreseeable future. Then attention shifted to the "special survey," which employed astronomical methods to establish further meridians. In 1875 the Second Initial Meridian was produced (106°), in 1877 the Third (110°), and in 1878 the Fourth and Fifth (114° and 118°). These meridians guaranteed the accuracy of further surveys in the uncharted parts of the North-West, so that inevitable small errors could not become cumulative and lead to serious distortion. The special survey also traced out the base lines and correction lines which were the horizontal axes of the great checkerboard.

Completion of the special survey made possible an extraordinary burst of surveying. The figures speak for themselves[2]:

Year	Acres Subdivided
1879	1,191,000
1880	4,472,000
1881	9,147,000
1882	9,907,000
1883	27,000,000
1884	6,400,000

The American system, with minor variations which need not concern us here, was uniformly imposed. The basic unit was the township, a square block of land six miles on a side. The townships were arranged in vertical rows called ranges, running north from the border. Each range was numbered by its position in relation to the Initial Meridian to the east of it, and the townships were numbered from the border northwards. Thus each township had a unique numerical code. For example, T.9-R.1W3 meant the ninth township in the first range west of the Third Initial Meridian (see Figure I).

Each township was itself divided into 36 sections, blocks of land one mile on a side, 640 acres or 1 square mile in area. These sections were always numbered from 1 to 36, starting in the south-east corner

Figure I
SIMPLIFIED SURVEY DESIGN OF WESTERN INTERIOR

Third Initial Meridian

Ranges West of the Third Initial Meridian			Ranges West of the Second Initial Meridian		
R3W3	R2W3	R1W3	R30W2	R29W2	R28W2
T5	T5	T5	T5	T5	T5
T4	T4	T4	T4	T4	T4
T3	T3	T3	T3	T3	T3
T2	T2	T2	T2	T2	T2
T1	T1	T1	T1	T1	T1

International Boundary

T = township
R = range

of the township (see Figure II). For settlement purposes, the sections were usually divided into quarters of 160 acres. Thus a code number like SW¼-S.36-T.4-R.1W3 provides, to anyone conversant with the system, an unambiguous designation of a position on the Canadian prairies. It was also possible to divide a section into 16 "legal subdivisions" of 40 acres each, which were consistently numbered on the same principle as sections were numbered within a township (see

Figure II
NUMBERING OF SECTIONS

31	32	33	34	35	36
30	29	28	27	26	25
19	20	21	22	23	24
18	17	16	15	14	13
7	8	9	10	11	12
6	5	4	3	2	1

6 mi

Figure III). Thus an 80-acre parcel could be designated, for example, as 1.s.1&2-S.36-T.9-R.1W3.

This survey system was the foundation of settlement policy. Regulations were stable until the years 1879-82, when they underwent several successive mutations because of changing plans for the Canadian Pacific Railway. This instability was particularly unfortunate for the people of Prince Albert and St. Laurent, for it came at a time when settlement was proceeding very rapidly. However, order

Figure III
LEGAL SUBDIVISIONS
SECTION

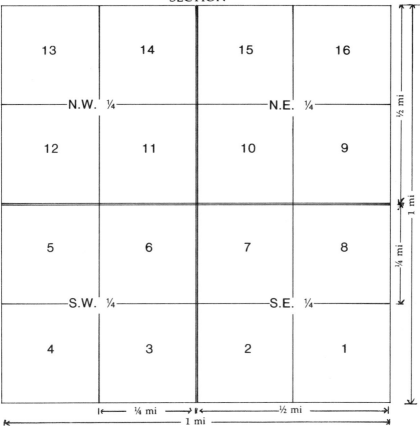

was restored with the promulgation of new regulations on 1 January 1882, which endured for many years. The land was divided into several main categories of use, illustrated by the model township of Figure IV.

(1) The Hudson's Bay Company was entitled to 1/20 of the land in the fertile belt of the North-West as part of the purchase price of Rupert's Land. This requirement was met by reserving to the company all of section 8 and ¾ of section 26 in every township (all of section 26

Figure IV
LAND USE IN A TYPICAL TOWNSHIP

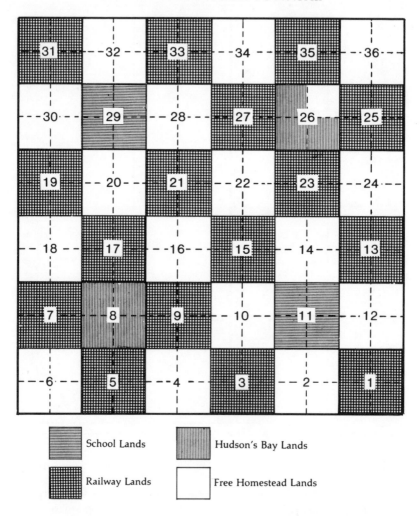

Source: Chester Martin, *"Dominion Lands" Policy* (Toronto: Macmillan, 1938), p. 233.

in every fifth township). The Company held these lands until it could find a buyer on the open market. In the event, most of the lands were not sold until the twentieth century.

(2) Sections 11 and 29 in each township were reserved as "school lands." They were sold on the open market and the proceeds were put into a trust fund for the support of public education in the North-West. The government disposed of these lands carefully, managing to get a high average price for them.

(3) Even-numbered sections (except 8 and 26, the H.B.C. reserve) were everywhere thrown open for homesteading; that is, the acquisition of "free land." Homesteading involved the following stages:

— making "entry" on a quarter-section through registration at a Dominion Lands agency and payment of a fee of $10.00
— performing "settlement duties," usually uninterrupted residence of three years, construction of a home, and cultivation of 30 acres or raising a certain number of animals
— obtaining "patent" or title after a Dominion Lands inspector ascertained that settlement duties had been performed.

When a settler made homestead entry, he could also enter a "preemption" on an adjoining quarter-section within the even-numbered section. Preemption was the right to buy those 160 acres at a specified price, once patent had been obtained on the homestead. The price was $2.50 per acre if the land was within a certain distance of the Canadian Pacific or other railroad, $2.00 per acre otherwise. The preemption was meant to be an incentive to the homesteader to complete his settlement duties.

(4) Within 24 miles of each side of the Canadian Pacific, and within 12 miles of each side of any other railway, all odd-numbered sections (except sections 11 and 29, the school reserves) were given to the railway company, to be sold as it pleased. In this way 25,000,000 acres of public land were alienated to the CPR. On the whole, the company sold this land quickly, rather than waiting for prices to rise over time. After all, its railway operations would hardly be profitable unless settlement proceeded.

(5) Outside the railway belt, the government retained all odd-numbered sections for sale at the preemption price. A variation on this theme was the sale of large numbers of odd sections to colonization companies, which could earn a rebate if they were successful in promoting settlement. Most of the colonization companies failed, and the government had to reach a financial settlement with them in 1886.[3]

(6) There were other uses of land which need not detain us here: Indian reserves, grazing leases, timber lots, redemption of the various kinds of scrip (half-breed, old settlers, military bounty).

This was a highly integrated system, easily open to disruption. For example, a settler who homesteaded in the wrong place might be depriving another homesteader of his preemption or might be occupying land to which the Hudson's Bay Company or a railway was legally entitled. The system could only work if its rules were generally enforced. Exceptions were possible but costly because they required so many adjustments to protect the expectations of others.

The system was, of course, imperfect in several ways. The quarter-section as a standard homestead proved to be too small in dry areas and had to be increased. Preemption engendered countless controversies and was eventually abolished. Financing railroads by land grants has often been criticized, and in fact it was ending in the United States at the time it was introduced into the Canadian West. The all-embracing nature of the system meant that it had to be centrally administered, which in turn meant delays as documents went from the North-West to Ottawa and back again. However, this latter point should not be unduly stressed. My impression after reading Department of Interior files is that the greatest delays occurred, as they do today, at the political level. The bureaucrats themselves seem at least as efficient as their modern counterparts. The most serious objection to the system concerns the concept of "free land." In reality, a homestead was not free, for monetary cost was replaced by non-monetary investments of time and effort. The system required considerable policing, as does any system which attempts to confer benefits at lower than market price. But the Canadian government felt it had no real choice in the matter if it was to attract immigrants after the United States enshrined free soil in the Homestead Act of 1862.

Even if there is some validity in these criticisms, the administration of Dominion Lands was one of the most successful government programs in the history of Canada. A huge territory was quickly surveyed with greater accuracy and at less expense than in the United States. The unified survey meant simplicity of granting and transferring land titles, which in the long run meant a minimum of conflict and litigation. In half a century, 200,000,000 acres were opened to agricultural settlement almost without violent conflict, the Rebellion of 1885 being the only important exception. A highly productive economy was created, based on the family farm and the free market. And at the end of this achievement, the federal government phased itself out of the picture, turning over jurisdiction to the provinces. Compared to twentieth-century interventions in natural resources, the administration of Dominion Lands was a masterpiece of government doing what it best can, creating a stable framework within which individual initiative can produce social and economic progress. It was certainly a system whose rules deserved to be enforced and protected for the common benefit of all.

However, it was not a system to which the *Métis* could easily adjust, for at least four important reasons:

(1) Literacy was, if not an absolute necessity, at least a great advantage in learning the rules enforced by the Department of the Interior and in filling out the applications for entry and patent. Most *Métis* were illiterate; furthermore, all forms and regulations were printed in English, while many *Métis* spoke French or some Indian language.

(2) The Dominion Lands system was meant for homesteaders who intended to settle permanently on land and support themselves by farming. Although most *Métis* claimed land and farmed on a small scale, agriculture was usually a supplement to their other pursuits. These varied with time and place, but included buffalo hunting, freighting with carts or boats, trapping, trading with Indians, and ice fishing. These avocations, often keeping them absent from their homes for months at a time, conflicted with the government's concept of continuous residence. Furthermore, the amount of land cultivated by the *Métis* when they were home was often short of the official definition of settlement duties.

(3) The Dominion Lands system worked well only when settlement was preceded by survey and opening of a land agency. It caused endless confusion to have to work around squatters. Yet the *Métis* were already in the country and could hardly have been expected to stop all movement for a decade while surveys were carried out. They aggravated this serious difficulty by continuing to squat on lands even after it would have been possible to conform to survey.

(4) The government's system was founded on the square quarter-section as an economically rational unit of land. It was indeed highly suitable to intensive, especially mechanized, agriculture; but it was unfamiliar to the *Métis* who had continued the long, narrow, river-front lots of their forebears from Lower Canada. This river-lot pattern was in fact well adapted to their way of life. The river gave them water, transportation, and easy access to the rest of society; the river banks gave them wood for fuel and construction; and the narrow strips of land were adequate for cultivating small gardens and pasturing a few animals. Thus the *Métis* would not readily abandon river lots in favor of residence on quarter-sections.

RIVER LOTS IN MANITOBA

The first conflict of the *Métis* with the Dominion Lands policy came in the new province of Manitoba. Although there were many irregularities, people had generally been accustomed to living along the Red and Assiniboine rivers on lots of 12 chains (792 feet) frontage and 2 miles depth, yielding about 200 acres. The 2 miles were often measured by sighting the horizon from under the belly of a horse. As the surveyor William Pearce remarked, "a good deal would depend on the horse."[4]

These claims fell into three different legal categories.[5] First were the river lots which had been expressly granted by the Hudson's Bay Company to settlers and whose titles were recorded in the Company's land register. These tended to be the most developed and cultivated farms, owned by the more substantial businessmen among the population, who were careful to keep legal documentation of land transfers by sale, gift, or inheritance. Second were lots which had not been granted by the Company but which were clearly settled and improved, with buildings erected and land under cultivation. That the Company had never tried to remove the occupants could be taken as tacit endorsement of their claims. Third were the lots, chiefly in the outer French parishes, on which stood the shanties of those who spent little time in the settlement: buffalo hunters, carters, boatmen, petty traders. The land might contain only a flimsy dwelling, inhabited a small portion of the year, or in some years not at all, and perhaps a little garden.

The different paragraphs of section 32 of the Manitoba Act tried to deal with these various situations.[6] Paragraphs one and two provided for explicit grants from the Hudson's Bay Company to "be converted into an estate in freehold by grant from the Crown." Paragraph three allowed for conversion into freehold of "all titles by occupancy with the sanction and under the license and authority of the Hudson's Bay Company," that is, those lands which had been permanently occupied and substantially improved. Paragraph four covered those situations where occupancy had been more tenuous. It provided that "all persons in peaceable possession of tracts of land . . . shall have the right of pre-emption of the same, on such terms and conditions as may be determined by the Governor in Council." This wording did not confer an automatic claim to freehold but left it to the government to find equitable solutions through administrative regulation.

After the transfer nothing was done about titles until the survey of the colony was completed in 1873, after which settlers were allowed to apply for patents. Generally speaking, farmers of the first two classes were successful in patenting their river lots in their existing dimensions, minus a strip of 120 feet parallel to the river which was expropriated without compensation for highways. But those with few improvements on their lots ran into a good deal of trouble. The government felt that large tracts of land should not be alienated for such claimants, who previously had shown little interest in farming. Claimants in this category received at most 80 acres, sometimes only a small residential plot, and often nothing at all. Although exact figures are not available, the only scholar to have studied the subject closely suggests that perhaps 1500 claimants were denied patent.[7] Appeal to the courts was not legally allowed. Furthermore, the government strengthened its hand by amending section 32(4) of the Manitoba Act.[8] The words "peaceable possession" were replaced by the formula "undisturbed occupancy," which the Department of the Interior interpreted as calling for visible improvements. Generally, the evidence of white surveyors, who may have had little comprehension of the habits of the *Métis*, was authoritative in determining whether improvements could be counted.

The great discretion vested in the Department of the Interior was an invitation to corruption. An enterprising clerk of the department in Ottawa, Robert Lang, conspired with two inhabitants of Red River to set up an extortion racket. Claimants who would give, say, half of their claim to an assignee in Red River would receive preferential treatment in the adjudication process as far as Lang could arrange it. The scheme was uncovered in late 1884 and Lang fled the country just as the claims from St. Laurent were to be processed. This caused some delay but at least allowed them to be handled by an honest man.

Vexing complications also arose over certain auxiliary claims. Most, if not all, of the older settlers claimed an "outer two miles"; that is, an additional two-mile strip at the rear of their river lots used for hay, pasture, and occasionally timber. In certain areas, where one side of the river was prairie and the other was wooded, it was common to reside on a river lot on the prairie side and to claim a two-mile timber lot on the other side. Another issue concerned "park claims," which were areas of indeterminate size on the prairie which some settlers used for summer grazing. Most troublesome of all was the problem of "staked claims." Before the transfer, some *Métis* had marked out lots along the Seine and Red rivers, as had some newcomers from Canada. Usually no one resided on or farmed these claims, which were identified only by stakes in the ground (hence the name).[9]

Roughly speaking, the Department of the Interior adjusted these claims as follows: patent was granted for park claims, which tended to be small and were numerous only near St. Andrew's. Where physically possible, the outer two miles were surveyed and patents granted. Those settlers who did not receive hay lots were compensated with scrip at the rate of one dollar per acre for each acre of land in the river lots on which they resided. This was not as equitable as it sounds because the government had allowed incoming immigrants to settle on hay lots before the older settlers' claims were settled. The government was not willing to eject these squatters, so old settlers who would have much preferred to keep the land had to settle for scrip. In the interim, many ugly confrontations between immigrants and old settlers helped to poison the atmosphere in the new province. Staked claims were settled on the principle that those who had actually settled on them would receive up to 160 acres free as a homestead, while others, including speculators who had bought the claims from those who had staked them, were allowed the privilege of purchase at one dollar per acre. All these matters took extraordinarily long to be resolved. The question of the outer two miles was not settled until 1877, and staked claims until 1881.[10]

The government's performance in Manitoba left much to be desired, although it may be going too far to agree with Douglas Sprague's recent argument that this government "lawlessness" was part of an intentional design to dispossess the mixed-blood population and drive them out of Manitoba.[11] The intrinsic difficulties of the situation, combined with the alternation of power between Conservatives and Liberals, account for many actions which with benefit of hindsight appear misguided or malicious. It seems unlikely that the government's treatment of land claims was, as Sprague implies, the major reason why so many Métis left Manitoba in the 1830s. After all, a similar westward movement took place among the Métis of North Dakota, where there was no issue of land claims. Indeed the entire Métis town of St. Joseph, Dakota, once a thriving community, disappeared in the 1870s.[12] The great migration had more to do with the social pressure exerted by the white immigrants, and the retreat of the buffalo, which the Métis hunted, and of the Indians, with whom they traded, toward the west.

PROBLEMS OF THE NORTH-WEST

In any case, the handling of river lots in Manitoba was connected with the North-West Rebellion only in the remote sense that it had engendered mistrust among the Métis who moved from Manitoba to the North-West. The specific problems of the North-West were rather different from those of Manitoba, even though river lots were involved in both cases. For one thing, relatively few old settlers in the strict sense resided in the North-West. The true old settlers — chiefly at St. Albert and Lac La Biche, and a handful at Prince Albert — were treated like their counterparts in Manitoba. Holdings occupied before 15 July 1870, even if they were of unusual size or irregular shape, were surveyed as settled and the owners were given patents.

The major problem in the North-West was the substantial Métis population in the North-West without a fixed abode. Their numbers were augmented throughout the 1870s and 1880s by migrants from Manitoba. Many of these Métis began to settle down, almost always on river lots, during the 1870s. They were not, strictly speaking, old settlers, and so their case was not provided for by legislation; but in equity they could hardly be expelled from their claims if they had settled before the land was surveyed and a Dominion Lands agency had been opened in their district. As most of the North-West was not subdivided until 1878-1884, many *Métis* did in fact settle ahead of survey.

The Department of the Interior granted these "squatters" certain rights by means of administrative decisions. Surveyors were given standing orders to subdivide the banks of major rivers like the Saskatchewan, Bow, and Battle, into river lots whenever they came upon a preexisting colony of squatters, usually *Métis*, who wished to have river lots. These lots were standardized to 10 chains in width and 2 miles in depth, yielding 160 acres (in practice the area might be slightly more or less than 160 acres, depending on the vagaries of the river).[13] A squatter could claim one such lot as a homestead and a second as a preemption. There were no outer 2 miles, hay privileges, or timber lots. If there were no settlers in evidence, or only a scattered few, the surveyors were to perform the usual rectangular survey. The decision was left to the discretion of the surveyor in the field, which created possibilities of misunderstanding. His estimate of whether there were enough squatters in a particular area to justify a river lot survey might not take sufficient account of *Métis* who considered themselves residents but were off freighting or trading.

The intent of these measures was clearly to treat the squatter as much as possible like a homesteader. Concessions were made as to the shape of the lot, but otherwise he was put on the same footing with respect to entry, settlement duties, patent, and the privilege of preemption. He was certainly not considered an old settler, with the right of immediate patent for whatever land he had occupied. Inevitably, however, the distinction between old settler and squatter remained obscure to many *Métis*. Having lived *in* the North-West before 15 July 1870, they did not appreciate the significance of living *on* a defined piece of land. They tended to claim the rights of old settlers when communicating with the government and were often dissatisfied with being treated as squatters. Yet it is difficult to see what more the Department of the Interior, in the absence of legislative amendments, could have done to accommodate them without creating an incentive for others to squat. The department was trying not to penalize the *Métis* for squatting without setting up positive rewards for such behavior.

This delicate problem was further aggravated by the propensity of *Métis* to squat even after survey had been performed. The department could not approve such settlement in outright defiance of regulations and was determined to draw the line at this point. It would not resurvey into river lots an area which had already been surveyed on the rectangular principle, merely to suit the convenience of illegal squatters. Cost was one factor: a river-lot survey was about nine times as expensive as the usual one.[14] Furthermore, it was desired only by the Métis. To create river lots to satisfy a few transients, who had flouted regulations once and might abandon their claims in the future, might entail still another survey to reproduce the quarter-sections desired by most settlers. But perhaps the most important point was simply the maintenance of governmental authority. The Department of the Interior had to administer a system which depended on compliance with rules. It was one thing to work out solutions for pre-survey squatters; it was quite another to accommodate those who had flouted rules. The Métis, for their part, showed little sympathy for this problem of rule enforcement. To the extent that the North-West Rebellion grew at all out of disputes over land claims, it stemmed from this collision of perspectives.

SETTLEMENT AND SURVEY ALONG THE SOUTH SASKATCHEWAN

Permanent settlement in Saskatchewan, apart from trading posts, began in 1862, when the half-breed James Isbister began farming on the site of what is now Prince Albert. Isbister soon moved to another farm, but settlement continued at that spot because the Reverend James Nisbet chose it in 1866 as the location of his Presbyterian mission. The mission became the nucleus of a town, peopled at first by Scots and Scottish half-breeds from Manitoba, later by numerous immigrants from Ontario. Outlying farming communities developed — Halcro, Red Deer Hill, Lindsay — which in turn encouraged the growth of the town. In 1881 the Dominion Census found over three thousand people in the Prince Albert district. All of this settlement had necessarily gone on without benefit of official survey or land registration.[15]

French settlement at St. Laurent followed a somewhat different pattern. Métis buffalo hunters had long been accustomed to winter in the area of Fort Carlton. The decline of the hunt and the urging of their missionaries encouraged these Métis to think of a permanent settlement. At a meeting held on 31 December 1871, and chaired by Lawrence Clarke of the Hudson's Bay Company, they decided to create a colony in the area. After a committee investigated several possible sites, they resolved in the spring of 1872 to make their settlement on both banks of the South Saskatchewan River for a distance of ten miles below the main crossing. This extended approximately from Fish Creek in the south to the great bend of the river in the north, with the future site of Batoche roughly in the

Figure V
TOWNSHIP PLAN OF ST. LAURENT AREA

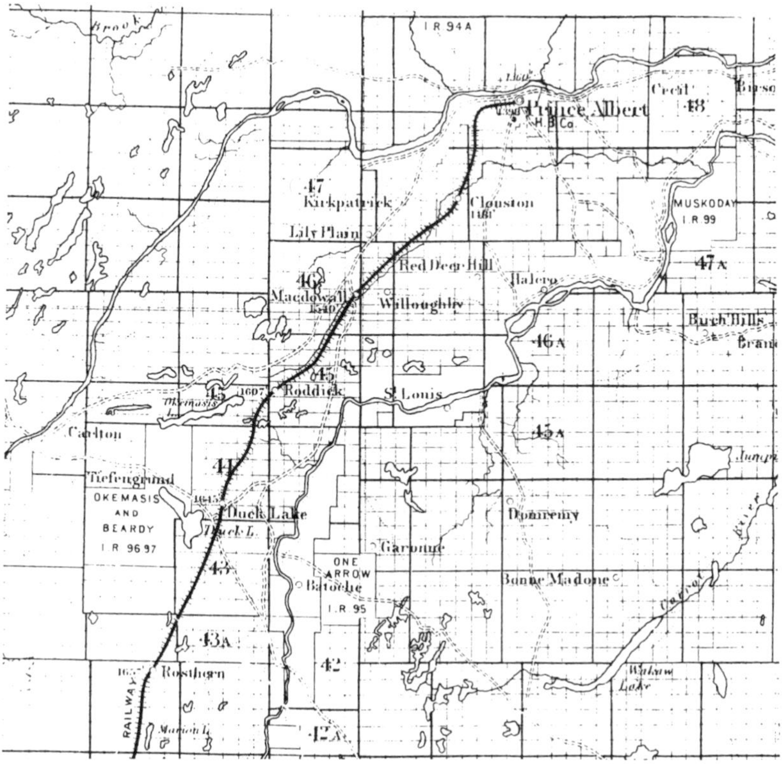

Source: PAC, National Map Collection, V1/502(1903).

middle.[16] Figure V is a map of this area of early settlement along the Saskatchewan.

Some of the earliest to settle were Gabriel Dumont with his father and brothers, and various members of the family Letendre *dit* Batoche. The church of St. Laurent was established at its permanent site on the west bank of the river in 1874, with Father Alexis André as pastor. Each year more *Métis* took up land, although in these early years they were often absent from their claim more than they were present. Father André's parish chronicle is full of references to the difficulty of getting the *Métis* to give up the nomadic life of the prairies. But the buffalo retreated farther and farther into Montana, and by 1878, according to André, most of the hunters had settled down and begun to devote themselves to farming.[17] As at Prince Albert, this meant squatting on unsurveyed land. The *Métis* marked off river lots for themselves, ten chains wide and two miles deep. Many claimed two or more such lots, hoping to homestead the first, preempt the second, and perhaps settle their children on others. There was no commercial center comparable to Prince Albert, although a few stores would soon cluster at Batoche and Duck Lake.

The government was aware of these developments at Prince Albert and St. Laurent; but under its policy of conducting one unified survey of the North-West, it could not subdivide land until the appropriate meridians and base lines had been produced. The special survey reached Prince Albert and established the Third Initial Meridian in the season of 1877. Later in the year, the surveyor A. L. Russell reported that block outlines had been done for townships so that both Prince Albert and St. Laurent could be subdivided next year. He emphasized that the people of both communities were anxious for an early survey.[18]

This sense of urgency was reinforced over the winter by two petitions of the citizens of Prince Albert calling for an immediate survey. "Disputes are daily arising between settlers with regard to locations and their boundaries; also between settlers and Indians, with regard to trespassing on their so-called reserves."[19] It was also stated that some settlers had taken river lots before 15 July 1870, and thus claimed "the same rights and privileges . . . as were reserved to the old settlers in the Province of Manitoba."[20] Interestingly, the *Métis* of St. Laurent submitted a petition over the winter, but it was silent about the issue of surveys.[21] Lesser density of population perhaps made such matters less pressing.

Surveying actually began in the summer of 1878. A party headed by Montague Aldous arrived in Prince Albert on 3 July to do the subdivision of the settlement. He carefully traced out 83 river lots, respecting existing boundaries. The lots were not of uniform size, varying from 57 acres to 315 acres (the Presbyterian mission). Where conflicts existed, Aldous tried to get the contestants to agree, with the result that they usually asked him to mediate between them. Where land was not yet settled, standard river lots, 10 chains by 2 miles, were created for future occupancy.[22] This painstaking work took the crew two full months, but it seems to have been worth the effort. Although the residents of Prince Albert would later voice many grievances, they never criticized the survey as such.

Having completed this task, Aldous took his men upriver to St.

Figure VI

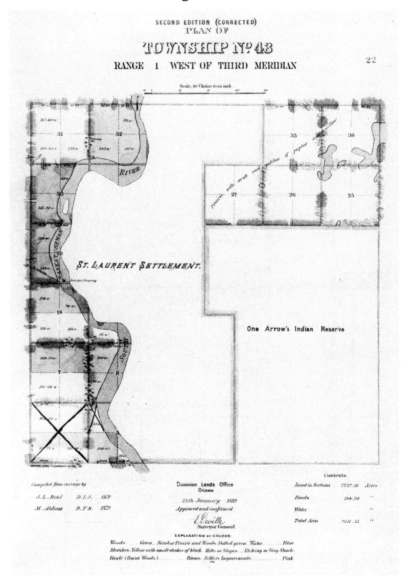

Source: PAC, National Map Collection (C112408).

Figure VII

PLAN OF

TOWNSHIP No 44

RANGE 1 WEST OF 3D MERIDIAN

Scale 40 Chains to an inch

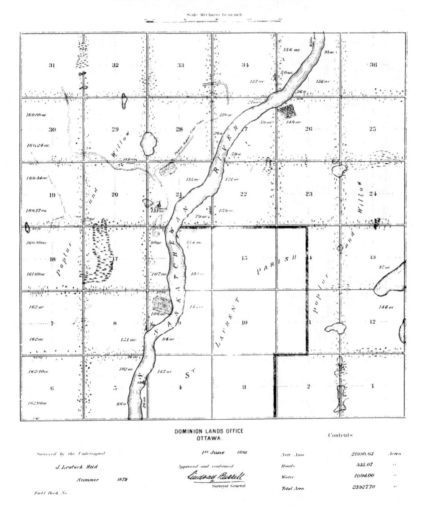

DOMINION LANDS OFFICE
OTTAWA.

Contents

Surveyed by the Undersigned

J. Lestock Reid

Summer   1879

Field Book No

1st June   1880

Approved and confirmed

Lindsay Russell

Surveyor General

Nett Area	20998.63	Acres
Roads	535.07	"
Water	1094.00	"
Total Area	22627.70	"

Source: PAC, National Map Collection (C112409).

Laurent on 6 September. Seeing that the settlement covered more than twenty miles on both sides of the river, he realized that it could not all be subdivided in the month which remained of the surveying season. Therefore he "determined to work that portion of the settlement where it was most immediately required." On the east bank of the river, he surveyed all of Township 43 and the southern half of Township 44. This amounted to a nine-mile stretch of river frontage, which was filled with seventy-one river lots, "conforming as nearly as possible to ten chains in width and two miles in depth."[23]

This excellent start gave the Métis exactly what they wanted. For unknown reasons, however, the work was not continued in the same fashion. In the summer of 1879, townships 44 and 43 were completed, as were Township 42 (Fish Creek) and several townships around Duck Lake. Everything this summer was done according to the rectangular system, even along the river banks. Thus only about twenty percent of the settlement of St. Laurent, within the limits understood by the Métis and by Mr. Aldous when he had been there the year before, was subdivided into river lots; the remainder was surveyed into quarter-sections.[24] Figures VI and VII show the mixed appearance of townships 43 and 44 after survey was complete.

The thinking behind this decision at the time has not been discovered. In 1885 William Pearce defended what had been done by arguing that there were very few families settled in the area which was subdivided on the rectangular system. Since they were few and scattered, they could conform without difficulty to the standard pattern. "The contention that the expense of a survey into river lots of that area should have been made to suit that number of settlers is absurd."[25] This argument, however, is open to serious question. While it is true that many Métis in the 1870s had not yet begun permanent residence, they had laid claim to lots along the river, claims which were respected by their neighbors. When the surveyors came to the district in 1878-79, there were undoubtedly a great many more claims than would strike the eye of an outsider. Regardless of the number of such claims, which cannot now be established with certainty, the Métis thought of the whole stretch of river on both sides as their own settlement. If certain lands were not yet claimed, they soon would be, and the claimants would undoubtedly want river lots. It was a serious mistake not to have carried on the river-lot survey in 1879 until the whole colony was done that way.

Another mysterious aspect of the affair was that it took an unusually long time to draw and confirm the plan of the restricted river-lot survey which was done. This process usually required one year, so that the map for St. Laurent should have been ready in the summer of 1880. In the event, all the surrounding townships were mapped and confirmed on schedule, but no plan of the seventy-one river lots was available until the spring of 1884. It was thus impossible to make entry during all this time. This was another irritant in the situation: even those *Métis* who had river lots could not begin the legal process of homesteading. The reason for the long wait is obscure. William Pearce claimed in 1885 that the delay was caused by a conflict over the boundary between certain river lots and One Arrow's Indian reserve, directly to the east.[26] The problem, which is discussed below, was real enough; but it cannot explain the delay from 1880 to 1884, because the conflict was not even discovered until the spring of 1884, after a map of St. Laurent had finally become available.[27]

An additional complication was delay in opening the Dominion Lands office in Prince Albert. George Duck was appointed agent and moved to Prince Albert in September 1878. He was able to give advice to settlers about Dominion Lands regulations, but he could not officially open the agency to accept entries until township plans were ready. Since much of the surrounding area was surveyed in 1879, and plans were approved in the summer of 1880, it should have been possible to establish the office in the fall of that year; but the opening did not take place. Appeals for a speedy opening soon came in from St. Laurent and Prince Albert. Father André wrote to the lieutenant-governor that a part of the property of the mission church at Duck Lake had been "jumped" by a man named Kelly. There seemed to be no legal redress, as the stipendiary magistrates could not settle boundary disputes without evidence of title, and such evidence could not be procured as long as the Dominion Lands office was not open.[28] Lawrence Clarke, now member of the North-West Territorial Council for the District of Lorne, also contributed a letter supporting Father André's request.[29] Whether because of this pressure or because of other reasons which are today unknown, the order to open the office was given on 2 August 1881, and the actual opening took place on 21 September of the same year.[30] Unfortunately this only became the prelude to more serious difficulties.

LAND CLAIMS IN PRINCE ALBERT

At this point, the problems of Prince Albert and St. Laurent, which up to now had resembled each other (early survey, river lots, opening of lands office), began to diverge. The very complex situation in Prince Albert will be discussed only briefly because it has already been thoroughly treated and because it ultimately had little connection with the Rebellion.[31] The problems of St. Laurent will be analyzed in more depth because they have never before been carefully studied and because they were directly connected to the outbreak of the Rebellion.

The difficulties at Prince Albert stemmed from the several shifts of regulations which took place between 1879 and the more or less final rules adopted by the Department of the Interior on 1 January 1882. Before 1879, it had been permitted to homestead on either even or odd sections, and the price of preemption land was one dollar per acre. In 1879, odd-numbered sections were withdrawn from homesteading and preemption, while the price of preemptions was raised. Less drastic changes were made in 1881, before the ultimate rules promulgated on 1 January 1882. The thorny question was, which set of rules was to apply to those who had settled before the lands office opened? Should it be the rules in force at the moment settlement took place, or the rules now in effect, which were on the whole less permissive to squatters? The complexity of such questions was multiplied by the way in which land had been transferred from hand to hand, so that a lot settled before 1879 might now be claimed by someone who had only recently acquired it.

When the lands office opened, the people of Prince Albert evidently received the impression that they would be rigorously held to the most recent rules (of May 1881). A protest meeting, quickly called for 8 October 1881, passed several resolutions which amounted to a demand to be treated according to the rules in force before 1879. They also demanded that the years spent in residence on their claims during the period when it was impossible to make entry be counted towards the fulfillment of settlement duties. Those in attendance pledged themselves to refrain from making entry until their demands were met.[32]

This petition received an immediate response from Lindsay Russell, acting deputy minister of the interior. He clarified certain misconceptions, made concessions on some points, and explained that in other areas legislation prevented him from acceding to everything that had been requested.[33] But the problem was not to be resolved so easily, for the settlers were persistent. Charles Mair and D. H. Macdowall went to Ottawa on their behalf in April 1882, where they interviewed the prime minister and prepared a memorial at his request.[34] Meanwhile, similar problems were arising in other districts such as Edmonton, Qu'Appelle, and Battleford, where settlement had preceded survey.

The government recognized that an equitable solution was necessary. Sir John A. Macdonald wrote to the minister of the interior in July 1882 that something had to be done about the claims of these settlers, "lest they all become Grits."[35] But instantaneous action was not possible for at least three major reasons: (1) Important questions of law, involving both legislation and orders-in-council, were at stake. The principles had to be worked out before the particular claims could be settled. (2) Squatters' and old settlers' claims from all of the North-West should be handled as a group, to ensure equity of treatment. Some areas, like Prince Albert, had already been surveyed, but others, such as Edmonton and St. Albert, were just now being done. (3) Matters had become so involved that they could not be settled at long distance. It would be necessary to send a commissioner into the field to take evidence respecting individual cases.

Late in 1882, the minister of the interior decided to release Lindsay Russell from his duties in Ottawa so he could go to the North-West to investigate these claims.[36] It was a good choice. Russell was a trained surveyor with many years' experience in Manitoba and the North-West. He spoke French and Cree in addition to English. Having risen to the rank of deputy minister, he could be entrusted with almost plenipotentiary powers to settle claims on the spot.

Then in February 1883 occurred one of those accidents which influence history: Lindsay Russell broke his leg. Hoping that he would recover in time to carry out his assignment in the summer of 1883, he continued to make preparations. In April he drafted a long memo proposing principles for settling these claims; it was approved by the governor general in Council in July.[37] The foundation for a comprehensive settlement was now laid, but Russell was still unable to go because of his health. He recommended at one point that his memo might be sent to George Duck at Prince Albert for implementation, because once the principles were worked out, the rest was a "mere matter of detail."[38] However, the government realized that things had gone too far to be resolved by a local agent, so the responsibility was transferred to William Pearce, Dominion Lands inspector.

Pearce, charged with investigating all areas in the North-West where settlement had preceded survey, commenced his work at Prince Albert. Arriving there with an assistant on 15 January 1884, he remained until 27 February. With the help of George Duck, he took evidence on every contested claim in the district, which meant collecting over 1,000 affidavits. He then returned to his office in Winnipeg, where he produced a report which must still command respect as a model of competent administration. A long introduction reviewed the history of the Prince Albert disputes and enunciated the principles to be followed in resolving them. The claims were divided into twenty-one classes, depending on the precise nature of the problem. For example, Class I contained the few genuine "old settlers" who had taken up residence before 15 July 1870; Class XII contained those who had squatted on lands which proved, after survey, to belong to the Hudson's Bay Company; and so on. Each claim was detailed within its particular class, with a recommendation by Pearce as to disposition. All were treated consistently under the same principles.[39]

Some of these principles can be stated briefly in a non-technical way. Each claimant was allowed a free homestead up to 160 acres. If he claimed more, he would have to purchase it at the preemption price. That price was determined by the regulations prevailing at the time he settled, not retroactively by regulations in force when the lands office opened. Residence prior to entry could be counted towards settlement duties if it could be proved by affidavits. Prior sales of unpatented lands were also recognized upon affidavit. Pearce noted with amazement that he was not presented with even one case of disputed ownership, which "speaks eloquently for the honesty of the settlers there."[40]

Pearce's recommendations, after being approved in Ottawa, were communicated to the settlers and they were invited to make entry on that basis. His work was widely perceived as just. There were only one or two appeals afterwards, so that his mission may be said to have resolved the grievances among the inhabitants of Prince Albert and the surrounding farming communities. This no doubt contributed to the reluctance of the white settlers and English half-breeds to join the *Métis* of St. Laurent when the latter took up arms. The people of Prince Albert had other grievances against the government, but they felt that their land claims had been resolved. The *Métis*, in contrast, felt that they had been denied justice in the settlement of their claims. To appreciate why this was so, we must return to the fall of 1881 and follow the course of events at St. Laurent.

LAND CLAIMS IN ST. LAURENT

The *Métis* shared some of the complaints of the people of Prince Albert, but to a lesser degree. There had not been as many sales of unpatented land at high prices, so not as much was at stake. Also, some *Métis* cared little about preemption, since they did not expect to have the money to preempt land, no matter what the price. But they had their own unique problem which had not troubled Prince Albert at all: the incomplete survey of river lots.

Passage of time only exacerbated the situation. After the seventy-one river lots had been surveyed in 1878, *Métis* continued to migrate to St. Laurent, the plains hunters being joined by substantial numbers from Manitoba. The biggest year for settlement was 1882, when fifty families arrived, according to Father André's estimate.[41] Some of the newcomers took unclaimed river lots, others took quarter-sections around Duck Lake; but many marked out their own ten-chain lots on river banks that had already been surveyed on the rectangular plan. This was especially prevalent at the north and south ends of the colony, which had been lightly settled at the time of the first survey. To the south, Township 42 (Fish Creek) quickly filled up with squatters on ten-chain lots. Also affected were the next townships farther south, which were surveyed on the sectional plan in 1882. In these townships some *Métis* managed to squat on river lots before survey, others did so afterwards. They seemed to see no difference. Another affected area was the north end of the colony, which received its own church in 1882, St. Louis de Langevin (so named by Bishop Grandin in a moment of euphoria over promises made by Hector Langevin, minister of public works).[42] In the area where the prevailing course of the river changed from south-north to west-east, the south side of the bend presented particularly intractable difficulties because there several squatters had crowded in on each other, creating bitterly contested claims. All along this stretch of river, land previously surveyed into quarter-sections was taken up as river lots.

The problem first came to official attention shortly after the Prince Albert lands office opened, when several *Métis* called on George Duck to explain the matter. Duck, always sympathetic to the *Métis*, wrote to Ottawa on 11 March 1882, to see if it might be possible to resurvey the contested sections into river lots.[43] When the answer came on 21 September of that year, it was negative: "it is not the intention of the Government to cause any resurveys to be made. Of course, any subdivision differing from the regular survey they may desire they can procure for themselves when the lands come into their possession."[44] This last sentence held out some hope of a compromise solution, but it was too vague to be of any use at this point.

While waiting for an answer to Duck's request, some *Métis* newcomers also composed their own petition, which they submitted to the prime minister. The document is quoted at length to illustrate one vexatious aspect of the problem: the *Métis* and the missionary priests who advised them did not have a good understanding of Dominion Lands rules. The petitions they submitted tended to misrepresent facts and to ask for things which an informed person could have told them would be impossible for the government to grant. The confused nature of these petitions probably caused them to receive a less than sympathetic hearing. The bureaucratic expert, confronted with a document full of palpable errors, might well miss the genuine problems lurking beneath the surface. The petition read in part:

> Compelled, most of us, to abandon the prairie, which can no longer furnish us the means of subsistence, we came in large numbers, during the course of the summer, and settled on the South branch of the Saskatchewan; pleased with the land and

the country, we set ourselves actively to work clearing the land, but in hope of sowing next spring, and also to prepare our houses for the winter now advancing rapidly. The surveyed lands being already occupied or sold, we were compelled to occupy lands not yet surveyed, being ignorant, for the most part, also, of the regulations of the Government respecting Dominion lands. Great then was our astonishment and perplexity when we were notified, that when the lands are surveyed we shall be obliged to pay $2 an acre to the Government, if our lands are included in odd-numbered sections. We desire, moreover, to keep close together, in order more easily to secure a school and a church. We are poor people and cannot pay for our land without utter ruin, and losing the fruits of our labor and seeing our lands pass into the hands of strangers, who will go to the land office at Prince Albert and pay the amount fixed by the Government. In our anxiety we appeal to your sense of justice as Minister of the Interior and head of the Government, and beg you to reassure us speedily, by directing that we shall not be disturbed on our lands, and that the Government grant us the privilege of considering us as occupants of even-numbered sections, since we have occupied these lands in good faith. Having so long held this country as its masters and so often defended it against the Indians at the price of our blood, we consider it not asking too much to request that the Government allow us to occupy our lands in peace, and that exception be made to its regulations, by making to the half-breeds of the North-West free grants of land. We also pray that you would direct that the lots be surveyed along the river ten chains in width by two miles in depth, this mode of division being the long-established usage of the country. This would render it more easy for us to know the limits of our several lots.[45]

The fallacies in the petition may be briefly indicated. It was allegedly written by people who had settled in the summer of 1882 on unsurveyed land. Yet all the land along the Saskatchewan had been surveyed by 1880, except for the northern and southern extremities of the colony. Many of the petitioners had not settled on unsurveyed land but had squatted illegally on surveyed land. The petition also asked for a river-lot survey without acknowledging that some river lots had already been created and that to create more would mean not just a survey but a resurvey. Finally, the petition asked in effect that all regulations be waived to allow the Métis "free grants of lands." No government could do this under the Dominion Lands Act except for "old settlers," which these Métis did not claim to be.

The response from the Department of the Interior was speedy and negative: "when the proper time arrives the case of each *bona fide* settler will be dealt with on its own merits; but as regards the surveying of the land in question, . . . all lands in the North-West Territories will be surveyed according to the system now in force."[46] The reference to dealing with cases individually hinted that an accommodation might be found, but did not offer any concrete ideas that the *Métis* could grasp. A more circumstantial reply might have steered them towards thoughts of a compromise; as it was, they became more adamant in their insistence on a resurvey.

It was now Father André's turn to write to the prime minister. On 16 January 1883, he composed a letter which was unfortunately as inaccurate as the petition of the previous September. The *Métis*, he wrote, had taken up river lots along the South Saskatchewan in their traditional manner, "expecting the surveyors to ratify their claims. Their surprise may be imagined when they saw the lands along the Saskatchewan measured off into squares of forty chains, without any heed being given to their just claims and protests." André drew an unfavorable comparison with Prince Albert, alleging that that city had received river lots whereas St. Laurent had not. "I cannot understand, Sir, why your surveyors should have two different methods of parcelling the public domain."[47]

The letter obscured the fact that many of the *Métis* involved in the problem had settled after survey, not before. The misleading contrast with Prince Albert also concealed the existence of the seventy-one river lots already surveyed at St. Laurent. Confronted with this misinformation, the perplexed minister asked his deputy, "How is it these difficulties recur so often, when it is the rule of the Department to survey around the old surveys without disturbing the occupants?"[48] When he learned the true facts, he perhaps felt the letter not worth answering; at least no reply has been found. Once again an opportunity to resolve the problem was missed.

Although Father André's letter had no visible consequences, the determination of the *Métis* to have their settlement resurveyed grew even stronger in 1883. When elections to the Territorial Council were held in March, the *Métis* put up a list of grievances including a demand that both banks of the South Saskatchewan River be resurveyed into river lots for a length of fifty miles.[49] Both candidates endorsed the *Métis* list of grievances; and later that year, the victorious D. H. Macdowall ensured that a memorial of the Territorial Council calling on Ottawa to do a number of things in the North-West referred to the *Métis* river-lot question.[50] This must have encouraged the *Métis* to think that persistence would eventually triumph.

Even more important was a series of events arising from the survey of St. Albert, the oldest settlement in the North-West, where *Métis* had lived for twenty years on river lots along the Sturgeon River. Official surveying of the region began in 1882. Edmonton was divided into river lots, while the people of St. Albert were promised the same treatment. A river-lot survey was actually started there, but when it was less than half done, the surveyor was ordered to Fort Pitt. It is not clear what the government's intention was, but the people received the impression that they would have to be content with a rectangular survey. A protest meeting in January 1883 selected Father Hippolyte Leduc to go to Ottawa on behalf of the residents of St. Albert. He was joined by Daniel Maloney, a politically active resident sympathetic to the *Métis*. The two delegates also promised to present certain demands on behalf of Edmonton and Fort Saskatchewan since those communities contributed toward defraying the cost of their trip. However, they did not represent St. Laurent or any community in Saskatchewan.

Leduc and Maloney spent much of March and April in Ottawa, making their case to the minister of the interior and waiting for a reply. They finally received a written guarantee that St. Albert would be surveyed into river lots. The actual document has not been found, but various reports of it made at the time do not show any reference to St. Laurent.[51] Yet the *Métis* of that area came to interpret it as a binding promise which applied to them as well as to their relatives in St. Albert.

How this happened is not altogether clear. When Father Leduc stopped for a visit at St. Laurent on his way back to Edmonton, he told Father André about the success of his mission. André's record of the conversation shows he was aware that Leduc had been representing St. Albert and Edmonton, but not St. Laurent.[52] Yet by the end of 1883 the *Métis* were citing Leduc's mission as evidence that the government had promised to resurvey their lands. This overlooked the crucial difference in the official perception of the two situations: St. Albert involved the first survey of already settled land, whereas St. Laurent involved a resurvey to accommodate the squatters who had not conformed to a rectangular survey done when the land was almost uninhabited.

Reference to Leduc's mission first appeared in a petition of 19 November 1883, drawn up by Louis Schmidt and signed by thirty-one other residents of the parish of St. Louis de Langevin, which occupied the northern end of the settlement where the river's course turned eastward.[53] This petition was given to George Duck, lands agent at Prince Albert. Within a month Schmidt wrote to him again to stress the urgency of the matter. A newcomer had made entry on the sectional system for a quarter-section which comprised part of river lots already claimed by older settlers.[54] This illustrated the insecurity of land claims which were not supported by official procedure.

Curiously, even as the Métis continued to agitate in 1883, a few of them, most notably Gabriel Dumont, his father, and his brother Isidore, made entry under the official system for quarter-sections fronting the river. These seem to have been exceptional cases where low density of settlement made it possible to enter a quarter-section without creating a conflict with another settler. It also has been asserted, though it is difficult to verify, that these entrants continued to treat their holdings as if they were two miles deep, perhaps expecting an eventual resurvey.[55] In any case, this handful of entries did not signify a break in Métis solidarity on the river-lot issue.

For its part, the Department of the Interior proceeded on the assumption that no resurvey would be done. In the fall of 1883, William Pearce met with Father André when he inspected the local land agency. He urged the priest to get the Métis to make entry by quarter-section, but he also explained that there was a legal way for the Métis to retain their unofficial river lots. This was the method of legal subdivision.[56]

Figure VIII is a simplified plan of part of Township 44, showing how river lots could have been recorded and registered through the method of legal subdivision. The dotted lines in sections 22 and 23 mark off legal subdivisions of 40 acres each, 16 to the section. Each subdivision was twenty chains wide, twice the width to which the Métis were accustomed. Thus a river lot ten chains wide and approximately two miles deep could be legally created by taking the north or south half of a row of legal subdivisions extending over two sections. Because of the irregular course of the river, it might be necessary to make the lot somewhat longer or smaller than two miles and thus somewhat more or less than 160 acres. For example, the river lot at the bottom of the diagram could be described as the south half of legal subdivisions 1-2 of section 21, 1-4 of section 22, and 1-4 of section 23 of Township 44, Range 1, West of the Third Initial Meridian (south ½ 1.s. 1-2, s.21; 1.s. 1-4, s.22; 1.s. 1-4, s.23, T44R1W3). Although cumbersome, the description was precise and legally valid. The lot itself was of the desired shape, although longer and larger than usual. Similarly, a slightly shorter and smaller than usual lot is shown at the top of the diagram by the sequence north ½ 1.s. 13-15, s.22; 1.s. 13-16, s.23, T44R1W3. In this way the creation of river lots could be performed in legal documents without the expense of a resurvey.

This solution, although feasible, had certain drawbacks which left the Métis unenthused. For one thing, they may not have understood all its complexities. But even if they understood it, they would

Figure VIII
REGISTERING RIVER LOTS BY LEGAL SUBDIVISION

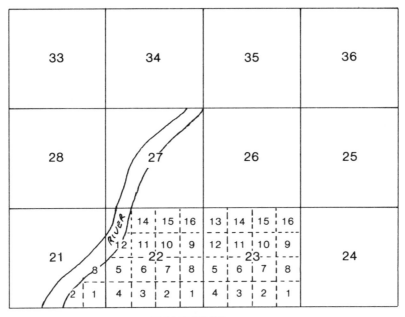

TOWNSHIP 44
R1 W3

probably have not been satisfied with it. Since no resurvey was to be made, there was no confirmation of their holdings on the ground, no surveyor's stakes to settle disputes between neighbors. The only proof of boundaries would consist of official records, a day's journey away at Prince Albert — not the most useful sort of evidence for an illiterate people. Furthermore, the river lots as taken up would not always coincide with the geometrically neat pattern of legal subdivisions. A squatter might find that some of his improvements, or at least some of the land he thought was his, would fall into a neighbor's allocation.

The *Métis* and official perspectives collided in January 1884, when William Pearce arrived in Prince Albert to begin his inquiry, which was also to include the St. Laurent area. Almost immediately, he was called upon by Charles Nolin and Father Valentin Végréville, who put to him their demand for a resurvey, supported by reference to the government's "promise" to Father Leduc. Pearce had to say that he knew nothing about this promise and that his authority to settle claims did not include power to order a new survey; he would make the best adjustments he could within the existing survey, which for the *Métis* of St. Laurent would mean the solution of legal subdivision.[57] Actually, Pearce, like George Duck, was carrying out a policy he had not made; he would have given serious consideration to a resurvey as an effective, although not the only, way to solve the problem.[58]

Father Végréville quickly wrote a letter of protest to the chief inspector of surveys, a fellow francophone:

> In February, 1883, Rev. Father Leduc and Mr. Maloney were deputed to set forth our claims to the Government. They were promised, in writing, that the lands we occupy should be surveyed as river lots ten chains in front by two miles in depth, and that the survey would be made in the following autumn (1883).
>
> The autumn has passed; winter is advancing; what has become of those promises?[59]

The various petitions and letters from Louis Schmidt and Father Végréville were forwarded for comment to Chief Inspector of Surveys Edouard De Ville. He proposed the method of legal subdivision described above.[60] This was accepted by the deputy minister, who instructed Pearce to follow this policy in his investigation of the *Métis* claims.[61] Pearce, realizing that this would not satisfy the *Métis*, wrote back that if a full resurvey was not to be made, there should at least be a rough indication on the ground of the boundaries between river lots:

> In reply, Mr. Inspector Pearce states that if he, personally, had time to make a survey of those settlers' holdings, he has no doubt that entries could be granted in legal sub-division or fractional parts thereof, so that each person's interest would be as well protected as if laid off in river lots, but that he has no time to do as that suggestion would demand, much as he would like that kind of work. He also states that he thinks, owing to points and bays on the river, it will be found that no rectangular width of lots will meet the wishes of those people, that their improvements are in all courses, that they seem determined to have their holdings laid out in river lots, and it will be found that they will expect the lines between every lot plainly defined on ground — at least, that is what Mr. Pearce states he inferred from

interviews he had with them. Further, he tried to explain to them
how their wishes could be met by means of a L.S. survey, or
fractional portions thereof; but he fears they did not com-
prehend what he desired to impart. In fact, it was a matter which
he took particular pains to discuss with others, and the better
educated portion of the community, and the answer invariably
was: "That is plain enough to you, as a surveyor, but it is Greek
to us. Those parties are *bona fide* settlers, as such have or will
acquire title, and if they wish their land laid off in a certain way,
why should the Government object? In fact, it is the duty of the
Government to survey it, as requested."

Mr. Inspector Pearce further states that neither the agent nor
his assistant are sufficiently conversant with surveys to go over
the ground and allot those lands by L.S. or fractional portions
thereof, and would recommend one of two courses to be
adopted: —

1st. To send with agent on the ground a surveyor who can
make a rough traverse of improvements on each section, and
then entries can be given by legal sub-division, so as to preserve
to each man his improvements, as far as possible.

2nd. To lay out in river lots on ground, employing a surveyor
of considerable experience in that kind of work. If he or his
assistant spoke French, so much the better; and give him
sufficient latitude in his instructions, so that he could make the
lots of such widths as to preserve to each claimant, so far as
possible, his improvements.[62]

Pearce's opinion must be accorded great weight since not only was he
a professional surveyor and a skilled administrator, but he also had a
first-hand knowledge of the problem. There is no evidence that his
suggestions were rejected, but neither were steps taken to implement
them. Had action been taken quickly, it might have reconciled the
Métis to the method of legal subdivision.

RESOLUTION OF MÉTIS GRIEVANCES

As matters turned out, Pearce himself did not conduct the
investigation at St. Laurent. The inquiry at Prince Albert took longer
than expected, and Pearce's mandate included other trouble spots in
the North-West. Furthermore, he did not have all the township plans
of the St. Laurent district. Just completed in Ottawa, they were mailed
in mid-February but had not reached Pearce by 27 February when his
work in Prince Albert was done. Also, he spoke no French or Cree and
so would have to do everything through an interpreter at St. Laurent.
All these considerations caused him to request and to receive

permission to return to Winnipeg to write up the results of his work at Prince Albert before going on to other places. George Duck was delegated to do the inquiry at St. Laurent as soon as the maps would arrive. Duck spoke some French and Cree, and having assisted Pearce in Prince Albert, he knew what to do. He was to gather the necessary information for Pearce, who would still bear the responsibility for formulating recommendations to settle the claims.[63] In retrospect it is regrettable that Pearce did not himself go to St. Laurent, but it was not an irrational decision at the time.

Duck wanted to go to St. Laurent as soon as possible, but he also wanted Father André's help, and the priest was not available until after Easter. Hence it was 2 May before the inquiry could begin.[64] Although Duck received partial cooperation from the Métis, they were still clinging to the hope of a resurvey. Louis Schmidt wrote again to the minister of the interior on this subject in late April,[65] and the point was made vehemently by Charles Nolin and Maxime Lépine to Bishop Grandin when he visited in June. The bishop then sent to the prime minister a letter, which, in contrast to earlier letters from other missionaries, was an accurate statement of the problem. Interestingly, this statement of the Métis position, which Grandin said was dictated by Nolin and Lépine, did not even mention Duck's recent inquiry,[66] illustrating the vast difference in perspective between the Métis and the Department of the Interiot. What to the latter was a decisive action to settle the issue once and for all was to the Métis an inconsequential errand which did not recognize their "right" to a resurvey. It may also have been perceived as a sign that the government was weakening and would ultimately give in if the Métis remained firm.[67]

Duck's instructions were to take affidavits from all Métis who had not yet made entry, including those who had settled on the seventy-one river lots and who had not been able to make entry because of the long delay in approval of that survey, as well as those who had carved out unofficial river lots on square-surveyed frontage. He was instructed to encourage the latter group to claim a standard quarter-section if possible, otherwise to allow them to claim a river lot through legal subdivision. No one was to be forced to give up land on which he had settled simply because he had not conformed to regulations. Each was to formulate the precise nature of his claim: which lot he claimed as homestead, which as preemption, which as purchase. Information would also be taken about the date of settlement, length of residence, improvements made, and other relevant facts. Since almost none of this could be documented, oral testimony of the Métis themselves would be accepted as evidence. The claimant would afterwards receive a letter informing him which land he could enter as a homestead, which land he could enter as a preemption if desired, what the preemption price would be, and what the price would be of any acreage which had to be obtained through outright purchase. The claimant might also be informed that he was eligible for immediate patent on his homestead if his improvements and length of residence were sufficient.

In the first weeks of May, Duck took evidence regarding ninety-nine claims.[68] This was a substantial portion of the *Métis*, but not all. A certain number refused to give evidence, and Duck did not do any work in St. Louis de Langevin because a large number of householders were absent.[69] This was unfortunate because the problems in that parish were especially difficult where settlers had crowded in on each other. Also, some of the most vocal spokesmen, such as Charles Nolin, Maxime Lépine, and Michel Dumas, lived there. If they had had a chance to state their claims to Duck (and if they would have agreed to, which is by no means certain), their subsequent attitude might have been more moderate.

Upon his return to Prince Albert, Duck prepared a schedule of the ninety-nine cases he had investigated. Thereafter his report had to traverse a long bureaucratic journey before action could be taken. It had to go to the Dominion Lands Board in Winnipeg, which in effect meant William Pearce, for formal recommendations. These recommendations had to be approved by the Department of the Interior in Ottawa, returned to Winnipeg, then sent to Duck for him to notify the claimants. Duck mailed his report to Winnipeg on 17 June,[70] and it arrived ten days later. But Pearce, who was off making other inquiries, could not do his part until the middle of October.[71] Further delays ensued in Ottawa because the "inside staff" was in disarray. Both the minister and the deputy minister were sick, while Robert Lang, implicated in the extortion scheme involving Manitoba claims, had departed for the United States. The hard-working, omnipresent Pearce was seconded to Ottawa to clean up the mess. Working with what remained of the inside staff, he arranged the approval of his own recommendations.[72] On 4 February 1885 the commissioner of Dominion Lands was notified of departmental approval of Pearce's recommendations, and on 25 February the agent at Prince Albert acknowledged receipt of the schedule of St. Laurent cases.[73] Between 26 February and 7 March, a letter was sent to each of the claimants stating the terms on which he could make entry.[74]

The delay was certainly unfortunate, especially since in the spring of 1884 Duck had optimistically told the *Métis* that they could expect results from his inquiry in a couple of months. In December 1884, Father André wrote to him that the long delay was causing "great discontent and bad feelings towards government among the french half breeds. . . . Something may arrive which will open the eyes of government when it will be too late."[75] He wrote this letter from St. Laurent, where he had gone to persuade Riel to leave the country if he could get some money from the government. Ultimately, however, the results of the Duck-Pearce inquiry were made known to the Métis before the outbreak of the Rebellion. Although the delay may have exacerbated hostility, it cannot reasonably be said that the government ultimately failed to carry out its responsibilities.

Let us look more closely at the treatment the Métis received. Many important documents are now lost, most notably the schedule of the ninety-nine cases and the final letters sent to the claimants; but enough material has survived in individual case files that the general outlines of the government's policy toward the Métis of St. Laurent can be reconstructed. The main principles may be stated as follows:

— no penalty would be exacted for failure to make entry before the inquiry of May 1884.
— each claimant would be allowed a homestead and a preemption of up to 160 acres each. Additional acreage would have to be purchased.
— the price of preemption and purchase would be determined by regulations in force when settlement first occurred.
— the time of settlement duties would be backdated to the point of first permanent occupancy; thus, if enough improvements had been made, it would be possible to make entry and receive patent on the same day, if the settler had lived there three years before making entry.
— previous sales of unpatented land, which had been very common even though technically illegal, would be recognized upon suitable written or oral evidence.
— although the area would not be resurveyed, unofficial river lots would be regularized through the method of legal subdivision.
— conflicting claims would be settled on the merits of the case (there were hardly any conflicts among these ninety-nine claims, although there were serious ones in St. Louis de Langevin).

Two examples will illustrate how these principles were applied: Calixte Lafontaine was a Métis from Manitoba. He had homesteaded once near Brandon and received a patent. Then in July 1883, he moved to St. Laurent, settling upon river lot no. 33, which was previously unoccupied. His oddly shaped lot, wider and shorter than normal because of the river's course, contained 176 acres. The recommendation was that he be allowed to take 160 acres as a homestead and to purchase the remaining 16 acres at two dollars per acre. He paid the money and received patent for the whole lot in 1889.[76] Evidence from other files shows that, if he had insisted, he could have taken only the free 160 acres and the Department of the Interior would have sliced off 16 acres for sale to someone else.

Philippe Garnot was a young French-Canadian from Quebec who kept a tavern near Batoche's crossing. In September 1883, he purchased for $500 a claim from Charles Nolin near Gabriel Dumont's farm. Nolin had bought the claim for $300 the year before from Pierre Vandale, who had lived on it 1878–82. It had been occupied as a river lot before it had been surveyed on the sectional system. The Lands Board recommended that Garnot be allowed to make homestead entry on this river lot, registered through legal subdivision, and to preempt an adjoining lot at the price of $1 per acre. Thus, although he had not become connected with the land until 1883, Garnot was allowed the preemption price prevailing in 1878, when Vandale had first settled.[77]

Many other examples could be produced to support the same conclusion: no *Métis* were forced off their chosen lands. They received river lots or the equivalent in legal subdivisions. As far as preemption and settlement duties were concerned, they were treated exactly like homesteaders at Prince Albert. Delay and confusion had surrounded their case, but in the end they received the substance of what they had wanted, even if there was to be no resurvey.

Duck's mission also uncovered a conflict with One Arrow's reserve, which lay immediately to the east of St. Laurent. When the reserve had been surveyed in the summer of 1881, forty chains had inadvertently been cut off the rear of lots 52–71. The surveyor drew the reserve boundary down a road allowance, neglecting to leave two miles depth from the river to accommodate the *Métis* river lots (see Figure IX). Although the *Métis* and Indians had been aware of the conflict, it first came to official notice during Duck's visit in May 1884. The affair was settled in November of the same year by allowing the *Métis* their full two miles and giving the Indians the equivalent amount of land elsewhere in compensation.[78] It is only worth mentioning here because William Pearce and other government spokesmen later used the conflict with One Arrow's reserve as a convenient rationalization for the long delay in approving the St. Laurent settlement survey.[79] But the correspondence shows that no one in government was even aware of the conflict until Duck discovered it in May 1884, so it can hardly be cited to explain the fact that a survey done in 1878–79 was not approved until 1884.

Duck did not include the parish of St. Louis de Langevin in his inquiry of May 1884. For unknown reasons, possibly because he did not have explicit instructions from the department, he did not investigate that area later in the year. In March 1885, the Rebellion intervened just as he received orders to proceed there.[80] After the

Figure IX
CONFLICT OF ST. LAURENT RIVER LOTS
AND ONE ARROW'S RESERVE

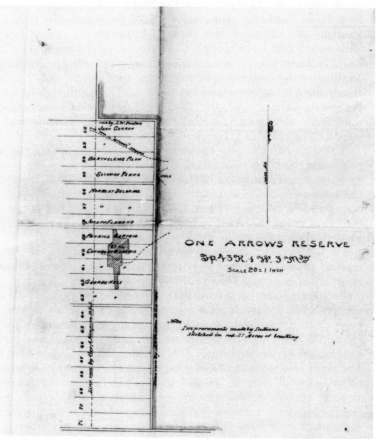

Source: PAC, RG 10, National Map Collection, vol. 3580, file 711, item 6 (12008).

fighting was over, Duck and Pearce jointly carried out the work. A report was submitted in October 1885, and quickly approved.[81] An example will show that exactly the same principles were followed as at St. Laurent. The Rebellion had no effect, favorable or unfavorable, upon the disposition of Métis claims.

Jean-Baptiste Boucher, a Métis from Manitoba, settled along the river in the fall of 1882. He carved out a river lot for himself about ten days before the surveyors reached that spot and incorporated it into the rectangular pattern. He resided there continuously until the Rebellion broke out, when he went to Batoche. A member of the Exovedate, he fled to the United States to escape punishment. His wife Caroline presented evidence to Duck when the parish was investigated. He came home 12 May 1886, after an amnesty was declared, and two weeks later made simultaneous application for entry and patent. This meant that the department was counting all the time since the fall of 1882 for settlement duties, even though Boucher was off his land for over a year. He received his patent later in 1886.[82] In how many countries of the earth would a man in Boucher's position have received such lenient treatment?

CONCLUSION

Let us try to draw some conclusions from this long and tangled story. The main problem concerns the opinion which is so commonly held, that the government was grossly at fault in dealing with the Métis of St. Laurent, that it ignored their just claims and procrastinated until the Métis were driven to rebellion. There is no denying that the government made some serious mistakes. First, it was an error not to have extended the river-lot survey to comprise the whole St. Laurent colony in the first place. Parts of it may have been thinly settled, but a little conversation with the Métis and their missionaries would have shown their conception of the boundaries of the settlement. Miles of river lots had been created farther north near Prince Albert in areas that were equally or even more unsettled. The comparison was invidious to the Métis.[83]

Second, it would not have been out of the question to resurvey the contested sections. The expense, although considerable at the time, would have been trivial in the long run. In fact, these areas were resurveyed into river lots in 1889–90 at the continuing request of the Métis.[84] Through the length of six townships, almost all of the east bank of the South Saskatchewan, and a small part of the west bank, was turned into river lots. If it was possible in 1889, it also could have been done in 1884.

Third, the Department of the Interior was plagued at times with administrative inefficiencies, which, though not individually serious, created a cumulative irritant to the department's clientele. These problems lay in Ottawa; the men in the field, like Pearce and Duck, were competent and dedicated. Examples are the long, unexplained delay in the approval of the St. Laurent survey, failure to get the maps of St. Laurent to Pearce at the right time, and the disarray among the inside staff in the winter of 1884–85. On the other hand, these inefficiencies should not be exaggerated. All bureaucracies have problems of this type, and the record of the Department of the Interior does not seem particularly bad, considering the magnitude of the tasks it faced in the 1880s.

However much one may wish to criticize the government, the picture is not nearly so dark as the conventional opinion suggests. The problems of the Métis were never lost sight of: from the time they were first detected after the opening of the Prince Albert agency in 1881, the department was always aware of them and trying to deal with them. The ultimate solution of granting river lots through the method of legal subdivision was a reasonable compromise, although it would have been even better if, as Pearce suggested, the Métis had been guaranteed some sort of evidence on the ground of the limits of their holdings. In other respects, the Métis were treated exactly the same as all other settlers according to legislation and settled policy. In spite of their fears, they were not penalized in any way for having settled ahead of survey and not having conformed to the system.

The Métis themselves, who are usually portrayed as helpless victims, must share some of the blame. They can hardly be reproached for settling ahead of survey, since they were already in the country; but beyond that they made little attempt to cooperate with the Department of the Interior. They knowingly squatted on already surveyed land in blithe confidence that they could force the department to resurvey it. One must also question how serious the agitation was for many of the participants. Indeed the claimants at Prince Albert were slow to obtain patents on their lands after Pearce's mission in 1884. Of the eighty-three river lots in the city, only thirty-two had been patented by 1889.[85]

An exact tabulation for St. Laurent has not been done, but inspection of many files suggests that the Métis were also slow to act on their claims, even when it became legally possible to do so. Many did not even make entry, let alone complete settlement duties and apply for patent. Moïse Ouellette, for example, resided with his family on river lots 11-14, yet did not make entry until the twentieth century. He died on the way back from Prince Albert, 15 December 1911, after having finally applied for patent on lot no. 11.[86] Philippe Garnot also did not act on his claim until after 1900.[87] The Dominion Lands inspectors apparently decided that they would just leave St.

Laurent alone after 1885, so many lots, probably a majority, went for years or decades without patent or entry.

The missionary priests, who were the *Métis'* closest advisers and link with the outside world, also bear some responsibility for the dispute. There is no doubt about their good intentions: they wanted nothing more than to see the *Métis* securely rooted on their own land. But they did not understand the complexities of the situation. The letters of Father André and Father Végréville were full of factual errors and misstatements which could only have weakened the *Métis* case in the eyes of government officials.[88] Had the *Métis* been better advised, they might have been less susceptible to the radicalism of men like Louis Riel.

William Pearce ca. 1880s.   (Glenbow Archives, Calgary, Alberta)

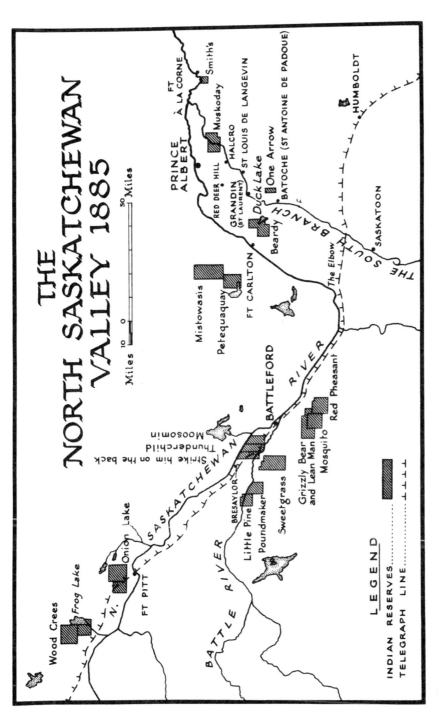

THE NORTH SASKATCHEWAN VALLEY 1885

Miles 10 0   50
Miles   Miles

PRINCE ALBERT

FT À LA CORNE
Smith's
Muskoday
HALCRO
RED DEER HILL
ST LOUIS DE LANGEVIN
GRANDIN (ST LAURENT)
Duck Lake
One Arrow
Beardy
BATOCHE (ST ANTOINE DE PADOUE)

Mistowasis
Petequaquay
FT CARLTON

The Elbow
THE SOUTH BRANCH
SASKATOON

HUMBOLDT

Moosomin
Thunderchild
Strike him on the back

BATTLEFORD

Red Pheasant
Grizzly Bear and Lean Man
Mosquito

RIVER

N. SASKATCHEWAN

Little Pine
Poundmaker
Sweetgrass
BRESAYLOR

Onion Lake
FT PITT

Frog Lake
Wood Crees

BATTLE RIVER

LEGEND

INDIAN RESERVES ....
TELEGRAPH LINE ....

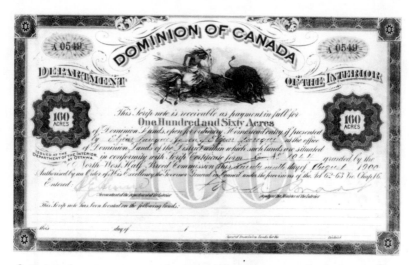

Scrip note for 160 acres issued to Elziar Laroque, Métis, 29 August 1900.
(Glenbow Archives, Calgary, Alberta)

Land claim in the name of Marie Rose Delorme, Métis, 2 October 1882.
(Glenbow Archives, Calgary, Alberta)

Bust of Riel carved by W. H. Jackson.
    (Parks Canada, Lower Fort Garry National Historic Park)

CHAPTER THREE

THE HALF-BREED LAND GRANT

The land question in the North-West had another important aspect. The mixed-blood people of the North-West repeatedly called for a land grant like the one provided for by the Manitoba Act to the *Métis* and half-breeds of that province. This demand was based on the view that mixed-blood people, as descendants of the Indians, had inherited a share of their ancestors' aboriginal title to the land. In the case of the Indians, that title was extinguished through treaties which involved surrender of their land rights in return for compensation consisting of reserve lands, annuities, and various forms of social and economic assistance. The land grant authorized by the Manitoba Act could be understood along similar lines: in return for surrender of whatever aboriginal title they possessed, people of mixed blood would be compensated individually with allotments of land. Once the precedent was set in Manitoba, the half-breeds of the North-West had an irresistible case for similar treatment. No one could offer a reason why their aboriginal title should be any less valid than that of their relatives in Manitoba. But for reasons discussed here, the government was reluctant to repeat a Manitoba-style land grant in the North-West. Parliament authorized such a grant when the Dominion Lands Act was revised in 1879, but the cabinet procrastinated in carrying out the legislation. The long delay irritated not only the *Métis* and English half-breeds, but also the white settlers in the North-West who looked forward to cheap purchase of the granted lands. The situation was conducive to the passions which are always aroused by a belief that one's "rights" have been denied.

Detailed analysis of this issue yields much the same results as in the case of the river-lot question. Mistakes were made on both sides.

The government erred once in gratuitously introducing the concept of *Métis* aboriginal title into the Manitoba Act; having done so, it erred again by postponing the extinguishment of the *Métis* aboriginal title which its decisions had created. For their part, the mixed-bloods, who everyone knew intended to sell the land grant as quickly as they could, inflated the issue with overheated rhetoric about sacred rights to the soil. Again, as in the case of river lots, the government conceded most of what was demanded immediately before the outbreak of the Rebellion. Though many errors and delays had ensued, the government finally did the right thing without threats of a violent uprising. Thus the land grant, like river lots, was a subjective but not an objective cause of the Rebellion. The problems surrounding it contributed to the discontent of the *Métis*, but the factual basis of the grievances was finally dealt with through the normal procedures of legislation and administration. While showing the numerous errors of government in these land-related matters, this chapter and the preceding one dispel the myth that the Rebellion was a necessary or justified measure for the *Métis* to obtain their rights.

ORIGIN

The troubled and contentious history of the half-breed land grant is at least partly explained by its origins. It was not something that had ever been desired by anyone, either the half-breeds or the Canadian government. It was born as a hastily contrived compromise in the negotiations of April 1870, which preceded the entry of Manitoba into Confederation; and it grew to maturity over several years of administrative efforts to implement an idea whose implications had never been thought through.

The insurgents at Red River had never demanded a land grant or anything like it. Their consistent demand was for control of all public land by the local government, whether conceived as a territorial legislature or a provincial government. This was characterized as a non-negotiable item in the instructions given by the Provisional Government to Alfred Scott, John Black, and Father N.-J. Ritchot when they were sent as delegates to Ottawa.[1] But such a concession was unacceptable to Macdonald. Provincial control of public lands in the West would have jeopardized his plans of railway construction and massive immigration under federal auspices.

The resolution of the impasse can be followed in the journal which Ritchot kept during the negotiations. He at first insisted on provincial control of public lands; but when Macdonald was equally adamant that this was "impossible," he softened his demand to "compensation or conditions which for the population actually there would be the equivalent of the control of the lands of their province." He was quickly able to get Macdonald and George Cartier to agree that all settlers should receive free title for the lots currently in their possession, but the negotiations then ran into trouble. The ministers wanted the half-breeds to be content with receiving title to lands in their possession; that is, to be treated in every respect as white men. Ritchot maintained that they had additional rights "as descendants of Indians" which had to be extinguished. The government's first offer was "one hundred thousand acres to be bestowed on the children of the *métis*." When Ritchot said that was far too little, the ministers raised their offer to 150,000 acres for adults and 200,000 for children. Ritchot's colleague John Black found that "very reasonable," but the priest, not so easily satisfied, countered with a demand for 3,000,000 acres. When his diary concluded on this subject, the final settlement was not quite clear: the ministers were offering 1,200,000 acres, he was holding out for 1,500,000. But a compromise was clearly in sight.

A highly significant point recorded by Ritchot concerned the role of the local legislature, which was to establish the rules for the distribution of this land grant:

> The land will be chosen throughout the province by each lot and in several different lots [sic] and in various places, if it is judged to be proper by the local legislature which ought itself to distribute these parcels of land to the heads of families in proportion to the number of children existing at the time of the distribution; that these lands should then be distributed among the children by their parents or guardians, always under the supervision of the above-mentioned local legislature which could pass laws to ensure the continuance of these lands in the *métis* families.[2]

However, this understanding did not find its way into the thirty-first clause of the Manitoba Act, which legally established the half-breed land grant. The wording of the Act requires careful scrutiny:

> 31. And whereas, it is expedient, towards the extinguishment of the Indian Title to the lands in the Province, to appropriate a portion of such ungranted lands to the extent of one million four hundred thousand acres thereof, for the benefit of the families of the half-breed residents, it is hereby enacted that under regulations to be from time to time made by the Governor General in Council, the Lieutenant-Governor shall select such lots or tracts in such parts of the Province as he may deem expedient, to the extent aforesaid, and divide the same among the children of the half-breed heads of families residing in the province at the time of the said transfer to Canada and the

same shall be granted to the said children respectively in such mode and on such conditions as to settlement and otherwise, as the Governor General in Council shall from time to time determine.[3]

Note that everything was reserved to the governor general in council and the lieutenant-governor of Manitoba; nothing was left to the legislature of Manitoba. When Ritchot protested to Cartier that their original understanding had been violated, the latter agreed that at least a local advisory committee, composed of notables like Archbishop Taché, should be appointed.[4] But this idea was never implemented, and the whole program remained in federal hands — not that the men in Ottawa had any clear notion of what they intended to do. Leaving everything to the governor general in council was merely a convenient way to postpone carrying out a plan which had not been thought through. This absence of forethought would hinder the execution of the land grant in years to come.

Improvisation was also marked in the stipulation that the land grant be divided "among the children of the half-breed heads of families residing in the province at the time of the said transfer to Canada." It was not clear whether the phrase "residing in the province" referred to the children or the heads of families, a distinction which could be very significant in dealing with the nomadic Métis. Even more problematic was the concept of "children of half-breed heads of families." This attempt to give an unambiguous definition of who would be eligible for the grant introduced a criterion which was completely foreign to the mixed-blood community. Under it, Louis Riel would have been eligible for the grant, because his father was a Métis; that his mother was a French Canadian was irrelevant. Yet Ambroise Lépine, who had more than Riel's one-eighth share of Indian ancestry, would have been ineligible because his mother was a Métisse and his father was a French Canadian. In fact, no such distinction was maintained among the Métis themselves, and it had later to be removed from the implementation of the grant.

The biggest error of all in drafting the act was to state that the grant was "towards the extinguishment of the Indian Title to the lands in the Province." These gratuitous words were in no way essential to the concept of a land grant to the half-breeds. They could have been given land as "original settlers," as was done in 1873 when a similar grant was made to the white Selkirk settlers.[5] The practical effect would have been the same, except that a privilege granted to original settlers out of expediency would not have been cloaked with the semi-mystical aura of aboriginal rights. As it was, the language of the Act established the Métis as an aboriginal people.

Realizing that an error had been made, Macdonald tried to undo the damage in 1885, when he told the House of Commons:

> In that Act it is provided that in order to secure the extinguishment of the Indian title 1,400,000 acres of land should be settled upon the families of the half-breeds living within the limits of the then Province. Whether they had any right to those lands or not was not so much the question as it was a question of policy to make an arrangement with the inhabitants of that Province, in order, in fact to make a Province at all. . . . That phrase [extinguishment of the Indian title] was an incorrect one, because the half-breeds did not allow themselves to be Indians.[6]

If these thoughts had occurred to Macdonald in 1870, much subsequent trouble might have been saved. But in fact in that year he defended the half-breed land grant precisely in terms of aboriginal title. "This reservation," he told the House, ". . . is for the purpose of extinguishing the Indian title." And again: "Those half-breeds had a strong claim to the lands, in consequence of their extraction, as well as from being settlers."[7] It was the Macdonald of 1870 rather than of 1885 who has prevailed in Canadian history.

MANITOBA

The story of the administration of the half-breed land grant in Manitoba is exceedingly complex, but it must be told, at least in outline; for the demand for a land grant in the North-West Territories, and the bitterness surrounding the issue, stem directly from what happened in Manitoba.[8]

The major source of difficulty was the obscure wording of section 31 of the Manitoba Act which authorized the grant:

> . . . it is hereby enacted that under regulations from time to time made by the Governor General in Council, the Lieutenant-Governor shall select such lots or tracts in such parts of the Province as he may deem expedient, to the extent aforesaid [1,400,000 acres] and divide the same among the children of the half-breed heads of families residing in the province at the time of the said transfer to Canada.

The text of the statute left many vital questions unanswered. Who were "heads of families"? Did the term include mothers as well as fathers? And who were "children"? The *Métis* often lived in extended families of several generations residing in one or more dwellings on a single river lot. Was a young married man with children of his own to be considered a child if he still lived on his father's land?

A. G. Archibald, first governor of Manitoba, had to confront these practical difficulties when he took office in 1870. He recommended to Ottawa that the land grant be conferred on all persons of partly Indian ancestry regardless of age or marital status.[9] Although this was undoubtedly the most sensible course of action, it was hard to reconcile with the wording of the Manitoba Act. Nonetheless, the government accepted his advice, and preparations were made to divide the 1,400,000 acres equally among the 9,800 half-breeds enumerated in the census of 1870. Each person would receive an allotment of 140 acres in the townships bordering the two-mile settlement belt along the Red and Assiniboine rivers.

After survey was completed in 1872, the allotment of 140-acre parcels began in March 1873. It was quickly halted, however, when embarrassing questions were raised in the House of Commons about the legality of including all half-breeds rather than just "children."[10] An order-in-council of 3 April restricted the grant to children, and the new interpretation was confirmed by statute the next month.[11] Since there were now only about 6,000 people eligible to share in the grant, individual allotments were increased to 190 acres. Some grants of this size were made during 1873, but the whole process was stopped late in the year and all allotments were cancelled. Technical difficulties had emerged because the townships chosen for distribution overlapped in some cases with the traditional "hay privilege" or "outer two miles" of existing river lots. Concretely, this meant that one person's grant of 190 acres might be on the same land as another person's customary pasture. Also, administration of the public domain passed to the newly created Department of the Interior on 1 July 1873. The new department wanted to have a thorough look at the whole land grant. Finally, Macdonald's government fell in November 1873 over the Pacific Scandal. The incoming Liberal government decided to suspend the land grant for a complete review.

Other complications had also arisen by this time. Even before the distributing of lands had begun, the *Métis* had started to sell their expected allotments to speculators. In an attempt to curb speculation, the Manitoba legislature passed, in March 1873, "The Half-Breed Land Grant Protection Act," which retroactively made unenforceable any agreements of sale concluded before the allotments were actually received.[12] Also, the legislature had requested that the federal government confer a land grant on the Selkirk settlers and their white progeny who could not share in the half-breed grant. In response to their request, Parliament, about the same time as it voted half-breed heads of families out of the half-breed grant, voted 49,000 acres for the Selkirk settlers on terms which included heads of families in the anticipated grant of 140 acres per person.[13]

(Incidentally, their land grant to the Selkirk settlers, although perhaps politically useful to create an impression of equal treatment for all groups in Red River, was without logical justification. The Scots were hardly an aboriginal people by any definition. They had been given land once by the Hudson's Bay Company and could homestead again on the public domain if they chose. There was no reason to give them additional free land. Doing so in order to put them on an equal footing with the half-breeds shows that the grant to the latter was less an extinguishment of aboriginal title than a political concession designed to buy them off.)

When the Liberals came into office, they were confronted with a double discrepancy in the treatment of half-breeds and Selkirk Settlers. Half-breed heads of families were excluded from the grant, whereas Selkirk heads of families were not; but half-breed children would get 190 acres, whereas all Selkirk claimants, adults or children, would get only 140. The whole untidy situation was resolved by new legislation in May 1874.[14] The half-breed grant of 1,400,000 acres was reserved for children, who would get 240 acres each. Half-breed heads of families, now defined to include both mothers and fathers, would receive their choice of one of two kinds of scrip: "land scrip," which was a coupon redeemable for any unclaimed quarter-section (160 acres) of Dominion lands; or "money scrip," which was a coupon redeemable for $160 worth of Dominion lands. The two were equal in value, since the sale price of Dominion lands was then $1 per acre; but money scrip was a more flexible instrument which could be used to purchase smaller parcels of agricultural land as well as timber, mineral, or pasture concessions from the Department of the Interior. The Selkirk claimants, adults and children alike, would also receive their choice of scrip. One benefit of the new system was that the amounts of 160 and 240 acres fit easily into the rectangular survey, which had not been true of the amounts of 140 or 190 acres.

Implementation of the new legislation was slow. In the summer of 1875, two commissioners, J. M. Machar of Kingston and Matthew Ryan of Montreal, enumerated all persons in Manitoba who were eligible for scrip or a land grant. Ryan continued for the next two years to take evidence from eligible half-breeds who had moved away from Manitoba since 1870. Meanwhile the actual distribution got underway. Townships were selected bordering as nearly as possible upon existing parishes.[15] The 240-acre allotments were written up in legal descriptions and then drawn randomly from a box for distribution to half-breed children. Most areas were finished by 1877, although disputed claims caused the process to drag on through 1880 in five parishes. In all, 3,186 heads of families received scrip, and 6,034 children received allotments of 240 acres (993 children, who had been missed for various reasons, received scrip for $240 in 1885). Eight hundred Selkirk settlers each received scrip for 160 acres or $160.[16] Undoubtedly there were some anomalous cases in which individuals did not receive their entitlement. Louis Riel, for example, did not get his 240 acres since he was in the United States at the time of the enumeration. He could not come to Manitoba because he had been exiled from Canada. There may also have been some cases of fraud, theft, or impersonation, as is alleged by contemporary Métis land claims researchers;[17] but even one of their most prominent spokesmen concedes that probably no more than 100,000 of the 1,400,000 acres for children went astray.[18]

This is not to say, however, that the half-breeds were suddenly converted into a class of landlords. They retained very little of this new land for any length of time: indeed most of it had been sold to speculators before it was actually received. This speculation was well funded and organized. Lawyers and bankers in Manitoba acted as agents for investors, some of them local people, others residents of Ontario. Speculation in half-breed lands contributed significantly to the fortunes of numerous Manitobans and Canadians, of whom Donald A. Smith, later Lord Strathcona, and Dr. John Christian Schultz, later lieutenant-governor of Manitoba, were two of the most prominent.[19] The agents followed the commissioners around the province in 1875, working from the same lists of names.[20] A half-breed could make his deposition and sign away his claim in one day. Money scrip was easy to sell as it was deemed personal property, not real estate. The grants of children posed more problems, but the legislature of Manitoba conveniently made it possible for parents to sell their children's allotments. The Half-Breed Land Grant Protection Act, which began as a means of curbing speculation, was later amended to facilitate sales. In the end, real estate received under section 31 of the Manitoba Act was exempted from normal rules which structured the conveyance of real property, particularly that belonging to minors.[21] All this was done not against the wishes of the mixed-blood population but at their behest, since they were eager to sell their scrip and allotments.

Few groups in Canadian history have been as consistently maligned as those who speculated in half-breed lands; but, in my opinion, such detraction is both unfair and irrational. The government price of agricultural land in Manitoba in the 1870s of one dollar an acre was a nominal price well above true market value. A homesteader could obtain 160 acres for ten dollars plus three years of residence and improvements, which amounted to six cents an acre in monetary price. The speculators seem generally to have paid about fifty cents an acre for scrip and allotments,[22] which does not appear unrealistic as a contemporary market price. The conditions of a competitive market were present: with so many buyers and sellers, no one could enforce a "take it or leave it" price. The condescending judgment that the illiterate half-breeds were ignorant of the true value of land and thus an easy mark for speculators is incorrect. The half-breeds may have been mostly illiterate but were far from ignorant of business. They were accustomed to bargaining and contractual relationships in selling furs, meat, and buffalo hides; working for the Hudson's Bay Company; taking business in their cart trains; and bartering with the Indians. There was a substantial bourgeoisie among both English and French mixed-bloods which could give advice to the less well-off. It was not that the half-breeds did not know the value of land but rather that they saw quite clearly that it was not of great present value to them. Agriculture was a supplement to their economy, not the mainstay. They had little desire to raise cash crops on the bald prairie; yet their scrips and allotments could not be located anywhere else, since they had already occupied all available river banks. Conceivably their children might have moved onto the prairie as commercial farmers, but that would involve a delay of years, which brings in the principle of discount. To compute the true present value of an asset which will not become productive for a number of years, one must discount its present nominal value by the expected rate of interest compounded over the period of time which will elapse. Another way of looking at this is to think of the discount as the "opportunity cost" of income foregone from tying up capital in an unproductive use. Assuming that allotments would not be used for ten years and that the average rate of interest would be five percent, the discounted present value of an acre of land nominally worth one dollar was actually about sixty cents. Speculators were willing to pay about that much cash right away in return for assuming future risks and benefits. All factors considered, it seems that the half-breeds made economically rational decisions in choosing to sell. Given their tastes and aptitudes, they would be better off by trading land for money to invest in other activities. Far from being villains, the speculators were benefactors both of the half-breeds, whom they provided with sizable amounts of cash, and of potential farmers, for whom they created a market in land as an alternative to the government's requirement of homesteading. This is not to condone speculation based on fraud or misrepresentation, and undoubtedly some such cases occurred, as they do on the fringe of all business activity. It is significant, however, that, although the existence of deception of the half-breeds is often alleged,[23] little documentation of particular cases has appeared in the literature. It is more plausible to believe that thousands of people making important transactions would not be simultaneously duped. To believe otherwise is to have a low opinion of the business acumen of the *Métis*, an opinion which would surely conflict with the information which is now accumulating about their economic role in Manitoba and the North-West.[24]

If anyone deserves censure for the outcome of the land grant, it is not the speculators but the government of Canada, which provided benefits in a form so easily sold. Yet it is not easy to see what the alternative was. The *Métis* themselves were insistent that they not be treated paternalistically like the Indians. They regarded themselves as equal to the rights and duties of full citizenship. It is doubtful whether any government could have long sustained a policy of paternalistic protection of half-breed lands.

THE NORTH-WEST TERRITORIES

Although the half-breed land grant in Manitoba is now decried by native rights activists for not establishing the *Métis* as a permanently prosperous landowning class, the main complaint of the *Métis* at that time was simply that it came too slowly. Otherwise, they seem to have been satisfied with the terms of the settlement. The half-breeds of the North-West Territories who had not qualified for the grant because they had not resided in Manitoba as of 15 July 1870 wished to share in the bounty. As early as 1873, numerous petitions from widely scattered points in the Territories began to request a repetition of what had been done in Manitoba, on the theory that mixed-bloods elsewhere in Rupert's Land were just as much aboriginal people as those in Manitoba. If the latter had a share of aboriginal title which had to be extinguished by scrip or land grant, so did the former.[25]

When he returned to office in 1878 and became both prime minister and minister of the interior, Sir John A. Macdonald took steps to settle the question. No land or scrip could be distributed in the North-West without statutory authority, so Macdonald incorporated into the 1879 revision of the Dominion Lands Act authority for the governor general in council:

> To satisfy any claims existing in connection with the extinguishment of the Indian title, preferred by half-breeds resident in the North-West Territories outside the limits of Manitoba, on the fifteenth day of July, one thousand eight hundred and seventy by granting land to such persons, to such extent and on such terms and conditions, as may be deemed expedient.[26]

The legislation was deliberately left vague because Macdonald wished to search for a new formula to avoid the speculation which had been the dénouement of the Manitoba land grant.

Macdonald had asked Deputy Minister J. S. Dennis to prepare a memo on the problem. Dennis reported in December 1878 that it was "expedient" to settle the half-breed claims "with as little delay as possible." Unfortunately, the Manitoba procedure was not a suitable model. "Indeed," he wrote, "it is anything but probable that a proposition of that nature could be again carried in Parliament." Nor was the Indian model of treaties and reserves appropriate, for the half-breeds themselves would never agree to it. Dennis's own recommendation was an elaboration of a proposal which had recently come from the North-West Territories Council. Each half-breed should receive a *non-negotiable* scrip for 160 acres which could be located on any vacant Dominion Lands, but special lands should not be reserved for this purpose. To prevent early sale of half-breed lots, title should not be granted for ten years from date of selection. Agricultural help in the form of implements and seed grain should be made available. If the half-breeds would settle in villages of fifty families or more, the government should also provide a school, teacher, and agricultural instructor. Finally, a system of industrial schools should be established to train both Indian and half-breed children in the arts of farming.[27]

Acting quickly on this advice, Macdonald appointed the Regina lawyer Nicholas Flood Davin to study American industrial schools as a possible example for Canada. He also had Dennis send his memo to several influential residents of Manitoba and the North-West. The Anglican Bishop of Saskatchewan supported all aspects of Dennis's proposal,[28] but Archbishop Taché suggested a well-thought-out plan which differed considerably from that of Dennis. Taché proposed to create twelve reserves, each of four townships (144 square miles), for about one hundred half-breed families. Each half-breed should receive two non-negotiable scrips for eighty acres, which could be located only on the reserves. The reserves themselves should be surveyed into the long narrow lots to which the half-breeds were accustomed, although they would have to front on roads rather than rivers. The lots taken by half-breeds should not be legally eligible for sale before passing "through the hands of at least the third generation." Governmental assistance in farming might be desirable but should not be offered across the board; inspectors should be appointed to discover where help was really needed. Schools would be important, but industrial schools would be neither necessary nor acceptable to the half-breeds. Above all, it was necessary to implement such a scheme without delay.[29] Other replies to Dennis's memo supported the thrust of his proposal but cast doubt on specific points such as the need for industrial schools or the propriety of government undertaking extra responsibilities in paying for local half-breed schools.[30]

Overall, this round of consultation produced agreement that the Manitoba experience should not be repeated but did not yield consensus on a practical alternative. The two main proposals, those of Dennis and Taché, were substantially different in detail. Taché's in particular was highly paternalistic; and it is questionable whether it would have been acceptable to the independent-minded *Métis*, who for their part were seeking a repetition of what had been done in Manitoba. Confronted with this dilemma, Macdonald procrastinated. When the Dominion Lands Act was amended in 1879, he inserted the clause, quoted above, which gave the government the authority to settle half-breed claims; but that is all that was accomplished. The Annual Report of the Minister of the Interior for 1881 claimed that "careful consideration" was being given to meeting the claims of the half-breeds,[31] but no concrete steps were taken until Riel's return to Canada in 1884 made matters urgent. If the government was at fault, it was not through inattention, neglect, or desire to take away the rights of the half-breeds, but through lack of imagination in designing a new policy that would avoid the mistakes made in Manitoba. Before criticizing too harshly, we should reflect that no one, in a century of writing about the subject, has yet said what the right policy would have been.

Macdonald initially continued to oppose a repetition of the Manitoba land grant even after Riel came to St. Laurent. He wrote to the governor general on 12 August 1884: "The land sharks that abound in the N.W. urge on the half-breed to demand . . . scrip to the same amount as granted to those in Manitoba. The scrip is sold for a song to the sharks and spent in whiskey, and this we desire above all things to avoid."[32] This letter shows Macdonald had abandoned his earlier efforts to find an alternative form for a half-breed land grant. Here he told the governor general that the *Métis* could either take treaty as Indians or homestead as white men, but he did not credit them with their own unique aboriginal title which had to be extinguished by additional compensation.

However, by January 1885, Macdonald had reluctantly decided that something must be done. Documents have not been found to explain this change of opinion, but presumably the reason was the increasingly serious tone of reports from the North-West about the temper of the *Métis*. Also, Riel's demand for an indemnity for himself, which Macdonald would not pay, probably convinced him that it would be wise to placate Riel's followers by authorizing a land grant.

On 28 January 1885, the cabinet, acting on the recommendation of the minister of the interior, authorized him to appoint a commission of three to enumerate the North-West half-breeds "with a view of settling equitably the claims of half-breeds in Manitoba and the North-West Territories who would have been entitled to land had they resided in Manitoba at the time of the transfer and filed their claims in due course under the Manitoba Act, and also of those who, though residing in Manitoba and equitably entitled to participate in the grant, did not do so."[33] Note that this order-in-council called only for an enumeration without specifying the form the settlement would take. It did not resolve any of the difficult questions of land vs. scrip, land scrip vs. money scrip, negotiable vs. non-negotiable grants, or individual vs. group settlement. It was only a tentative first step toward a policy.

It has often been said that, because the order-in-council was only a first step toward conceding the claim of the Métis, it was just one more meaningless "promise" which the government might conveniently forget. However, this objection misses the mark. The government was well aware of and concerned about public opinion in the North-West, not only among the Métis but among the many white settlers who stood poised to speculate in scrip as soon as it was distributed. It would have been politically embarrassing to appoint a commission, send it to the North-West, enumerate thousands of claimants, and then fail to produce a land grant of some kind. The government was still confused about many details, but there is no evidence it was dealing in bad faith at this point. Ironically, however, the peculiar way in which this conciliatory gesture was communicated to the Métis would permit its real meaning to be obscured. Sir John A. Macdonald, the consummate politician, did not take the Métis seriously enough to give any thought to developing a political strategy of placating them; he seems to have thought the administrative decision of the cabinet to order an enumeration would be enough in itself. But he neglected the truism that in political matters subjective perception of reality is at least as important as objective facts.

The minister of the interior telegraphed the news to Governor Dewdney on 4 February: "Government has decided to investigate claims of half-breeds and with that view has directed enumeration of those who did not participate in grant under Manitoba Act — no representation received recently."[34] Dewdney then acted with extraordinarily bad judgment. The politic course of action would have been to send to St. Laurent a French-speaking emissary, such as A.-E. Forget, secretary of the North-West Council, to explain that the government had acceded to one of the major demands of the Métis. The latter could have taken the opportunity to offer advice about the form in which they wished compensation to be paid. Riel, whose vision of aboriginal title went far beyond a paltry 160 or 240 acres, might have tried to impede discussion; but he would have been opposed by the missionaries. Instead, Dewdney sent a copy of the telegram to Charles Nolin, probably in the mistaken belief that making Nolin the bearer of good news would undercut Riel. All it accomplished was to enrage Riel, who first saw the telegram after mass on 8 February. According to Father Fourmond, who witnessed the scene, Riel exclaimed: "Ottawa will have my answer in forty days!"[35] The Provisional Government was in fact declared on 19 March, forty days afterward. According to Nolin, Riel cried that "it was 400 years that the English had been robbing, and that it was time to put a stop to it."[36] Both accounts emphasize that reception of the telegram was the crucial step in the progression from constitutional agitation to armed insurrection.

How to explain the paradox that a conciliatory gesture provoked such a violent response? The answer can only be found in examination of Riel's true goals, which were a massive settlement of aboriginal claims and a large indemnity for himself. The telegram, which was silent about both, was a signal to him that his peaceful strategy had failed and that he would have to resort to more radical methods. The bungled way in which Dewdney chose to communicate with the Métis made it easy for Riel to carry them with him. The cryptic telegram, of which he made himself the interpreter, became evidence of the government's refusal to deal with the Métis — the exact opposite of its intended meaning. However, even if the government made a serious error of judgment in the way it communicated with the Métis, it is definitely not true, as is so often alleged, that the Métis had to rise in arms to obtain their rights. The truth, illogical as it may seem, is almost the opposite. The government, fearing the Métis might rise, decided to concede one of their chief demands; after receiving the news, the Métis rose anyway.

Another fact which must be taken into account in weighing the connection between the land grant and the Rebellion is that there were extraordinarily few claimants for scrip in the area where fighting broke out. Although more than three thousand scrips were granted in the North-West as a whole in 1885-86, only 15 adult Métis men and 52 women and children appeared before the Half-Breed Commission when it sat at Duck Lake and Batoche after the end of hostilities. The number of men was somewhat reduced because some potential claimants had fled after the Rebellion, but it would have been small in any case. The surveyor William Pearce investigated the claims of 258 heads of families living along this stretch of the South Saskatchewan River. Of these, 175 were definitely Manitoba Métis who had participated in the Manitoba land grant and had no claim to share in a grant to the half-breeds of the North-West. Of the remaining 63 heads of families, many were American half-breeds, treaty-taking half-breeds not eligible for scrip, or not half-breeds at all. It seems likely that only about ten percent, or even less, of the population of the St. Laurent colony in its broadest extent had a claim to scrip as North-West half-breeds.[37] Without denying their importance, the claims of this minority must be kept in perspective when assessing the causes of the Rebellion.

The subsequent history of the half-breed grant can be briefly told. The government secured the services of the three commissioners — William Street, an Ontario lawyer; Roger Goulet, a St. Boniface surveyor; and A.-E. Forget, secretary to the Territorial Council. Street, the chairman of the commission, went to Ottawa on 25 March to receive his instructions from the Department of the Interior. He was there two days later when word of the fight at Duck Lake reached the capital by telegraph. In spite of the outbreak of violence, the government wished to push ahead with its project. Street suggested to the prime minister that, under the circumstances, it would be wise to empower the commission to grant allotments on the spot, instead of merely making an enumeration, as had originally been envisioned.[38] Sir John agreed, and the commission was in the field by early April. Almost immediately they found that the cabinet had equipped them with faulty instructions. The order-in-council of 30 March, under which they were to operate, specified that each half-breed head of family resident in the North-West prior to 15 July 1870 would receive an unconditional grant of title to "the lot or portion of land of which he is at the present time in *bona fide* and undisputed occupation by virtue of residence upon the cultivation thereof, to the extent of one hundred and sixty acres."[39] If his lot were smaller than 160 acres, the difference would be made up in scrip redeemable at one dollar per acre. Similar provisions were made for children of half-breed heads of families born before 15 July 1870, except that they could claim up to 240 acres free and would receive scrip to make up that amount if they had not occupied so much land.

These instructions were almost incredibly defective if, as was said, they were meant to confer upon the half-breeds of the North-West the same benefits enjoyed by those in Manitoba. In that province, the half-breeds had received title to lands already occupied *plus* scrip or an allotment of land. This order-in-council merged the two rights so that if a half-breed already occupied 160 acres of land, he would get no scrip at all, being treated in effect like a white man with no aboriginal right to be extinguished. Nor did these regulations do anything for half-breed wives and mothers in the North-West even though their counterparts had received scrip in Manitoba.

The commissioners realized the problem as soon as they reached Winnipeg and conferred with William Pearce. Commissioner Street wrote at once to the minister of the interior requesting the authority "to allow the half-breed to claim the land occupied by him under the homestead provisions, and in addition to give him his scrip for the $160, or $240, as the case may be, for his Indian title."[40] Showing that the error had arisen through inadvertence rather than malice, the minister replied immediately by telegram: "No objection to your suggestion to give scrip, and allow occupants to acquire title through possession when desired by them."[41] Curiously, the order-in-council was never amended, so that the distribution which took place may have been of dubious legality.[42] The commission worked hard during 1885; but the *Métis* were so scattered in small settlements over the North-West, and the Rebellion interrupted transportation so gravely, that their mandate had to be extended to hear claims through 1887.

Interestingly, when the commission met with a deputation of influential *Métis* at Qu'Appelle, they were told that children would not accept money scrip but would insist upon land scrip.[43] After having received permission from the minister to offer land scrip, they later found that it was refused by most *Métis* who overwhelmingly preferred money scrip. Of 3,247 claims eventually allowed, only twelve percent (394) were for land scrip.[44] Since all claimants, even "children," had been born before 15 July 1870, this figure represents the result of free choice, not of children being exploited by parents. Regardless of what was said by *Métis* spokesmen, the *Métis* themselves wanted their bounty in as negotiable a form as possible.

Much the same thing happened in 1899, when there was a distribution of half-breed scrip in the Mackenzie Valley in connection with Treaty No. 8. Clifford Sifton, minister of the interior, had changed the scrip documents so that, no longer payable to bearer, they required a legal assignment for transfer. The *Métis* refused to accept this scrip because the buyers who unofficially accompanied the commission would pay little or nothing for it. Acting on their own authority, the commissioners rewrote the scrip to make it payable to bearer. The *Métis* happily accepted it, sold it forthwith, and voted Liberal in the next election.[45]

The *Métis* who received scrip in 1885-86 sold it exactly as their predecessors had done in Manitoba. According to Chairman Street, the first recipient of scrip, a *Métisse* named Madeleine Hamlin, sold it immediately for $80 to a buyer from a Winnipeg bank who was following the Commission. The *Métis* at Qu'Appelle, who had considerable sympathy for Riel, had initially been reluctant to accept the scrip, but the appearance of money changed their attitude. "The news quickly spread that we were really giving something that could be turned into cash, and from that hour we were besieged from morning till night by applicants."[46] Similar scenes took place elsewhere. "Almost all of our people are taking money scrips,", lamented the missionaries of St. Albert in 1885.[47] Near Wood Mountain (Willow Bunch) the French-Canadian trader Jean-Louis Légaré bought forty-five Métis scrips for $140 each. They were said to be worth $1,000 apiece by 1900.[48] Yet for the same rational economic reasons as in Manitoba, the Métis preferred immediate cash.

It is a serious error to think of this whole episode as having much to do with a desire for land on the part of the Métis. They already lived on land, and their children, by homesteading, could get as much land as they could use. The Métis wanted money and successfully exerted political pressure to get it. This point must be emphasized because the almost mystical character which land has assumed in contemporary native politics tends to throw an anachronistic haze of distortion over the motives of the Métis in 1884-85.

CHAPTER FOUR

ABORIGINAL TITLE

Why then did the North-West Rebellion occur at all, if the objective grievances of the *Métis* were remedied by the government? In this connection, it must be remembered that many other factors contributed to the *Métis'* sense of alienation. They were still bitter over the events in Manitoba, which, in spite of the seeming success of the movement of 1869-70, had left them a marginal minority in their own homeland. Having moved farther west to escape this status, they could see themselves once again faced with being outnumbered by white settlers. Another long-range consideration was the decline of the *Métis* economy. The buffalo withdrew from the Canadian prairies during the 1870s and vanished altogether after 1878, adversely affecting numerous trades in which the *Métis* had been prominent: buffalo hunting, trading with the Indians for pemmican and robes, and transporting these goods to market. The *Métis* cart trains and boat brigades also suffered from the advent of railways and steamboats in the Canadian West. Deprived of much of the income from traditional occupations, the *Métis* had to rely more on agriculture. As they began to make this transition, they were struck, as were all western farmers, by the economic depression and fall in grain prices which began in 1883. For the *Métis* of St. Laurent, this economic malaise was aggravated by the decision to build the Canadian Pacific Railway along the southern route through Regina instead of along the northern route through Prince Albert. The *Métis* lost out on the jobs and contracts that would have been created by a construction boom in northern Saskatchewan.

All these factors help to explain the prevailing mood in St. Laurent, yet none really accounts for the outbreak of the Rebellion; for similar factors were equally at work in other Métis settlements which did not turn to violence. The unique fact about St. Laurent was the presence of Louis Riel. His great prestige made him a prism through which all information from the outside world was refracted to the Métis. His interpretation of the government's concessions made them seem like provocations. Any explanation of why the rising occurred must focus on Riel. What motivated him to take up arms? Such questions can never be answered with total certainty, but one can make a reasonable estimation of the forces at work in his mind at this time.

First was Riel's brooding resentment over the aftermath of 1869-70. Thinking himself the natural leader of his people, he had expected a quick amnesty followed by a successful career in politics. Instead he received exile, loss of his Commons seat, and penniless obscurity. His own misfortunes paralleled those of the Métis as they were submerged in Manitoba politics and went into voluntary emigration. Riel's bitterness lay behind the efforts he would make in the winter of 1884-85 to obtain a cash payment from the federal government (see the next chapter). In his mind, this was fair compensation for the wrongs he had suffered. The failure of these efforts to show any tangible result must have strengthened his readiness to undertake extreme measures.

A second factor was Riel's religious "mission." As I have shown at length in Louis "David" Riel: "Prophet of the New World," he believed himself to be a divinely inspired prophet, even after his "cure" in the insane asylums of Quebec. His mission of religious reform was only in abeyance, awaiting a signal from God to be made public. The longer he stayed with the Métis, the more ostentatious became Riel's piety. He began to argue with the Oblate missionaries over points of politics and theology, until the exasperated priests threatened him with excommunication. The notebook of prayers he kept over the winter of 1884-85 shows an ascending curve of spiritual confidence culminating in readiness for action. Riel launched the Rebellion convinced it was the occasion to reveal his new religion to the world. That is why he began his first major speech to the Métis with the words, "Rome has fallen."

In spite of this religious dimension, Riel's rising was a political phenomenon whose causes must also be sought at the political level. If the Métis grievances over river lots and land scrip do not furnish an adequate explanation, more insight can be found through examining Riel's views on aboriginal rights. For reasons explained below, he held that the Métis were the true owners of the North-West; that their entry into Confederation had been conditional upon fulfillment of the Manitoba "treaty"; and that they were legally and morally free to secede from Canada since (in his view) the "treaty" had not been kept by Canada. In this sweeping perspective, the grievances of river lots and scrip were petty complaints, useful in mobilizing local support but peripheral to the real issues. Study of the course of the agitation, from July 1884, when Riel arrived at St. Laurent, to February 1885, the eve of the Rebellion, demonstrates that his strategy was built upon his radical view of aboriginal rights. Preexisting local grievances were only pawns in a complex series of maneuvers aimed at vindicating *Métis* ownership of the North-West as a whole. To understand this is to explain the apparent paradox that the *Métis* launched an insurrection immediately after the government granted their demands. Under Riel's leadership, they were fighting for stakes which far transcended river lots and scrip. They may have only dimly perceived what the real goals were, but these are plain enough in Riel's writings.

CONFLICTING VIEWS OF ABORIGINAL RIGHTS

Riel's political views can only be appreciated against the background of the events of 1869-70 and their aftermath. In his interpretation of these events he was quite different from official circles in Ottawa or London. To see the magnitude of this difference, we must first sketch the official view. Here, a word of caution is required. What I call the "official view" was not articulated until the *St. Catherine's Milling Case*, decided in 1889. But the theory of aboriginal rights developed in this case was, I believe, implicit in the practice of the previous decades, including the acquisition of Rupert's Land by Canada and subsequent dealings with Indians and half-breeds in that territory. Naturally, there is room for debate over the exact contours of an implicit, unarticulated view.

To the rulers of Britain and Canada as well as to the proprietors of the Hudson's Bay Company, the acquisition by Canada of Rupert's Land and the Northwestern Territories was a complicated real estate conveyance. In return for compensation from Canada, the Company surrendered its land to the Crown, which in turn passed it to Canada by Act of Parliament and Royal Proclamation. The transaction was founded on the property rights conferred on the Company by the royal charter of 1670:

> . . . the sole trade and commerce of all those seas, straights, bays, rivers, creeks and sounds in whatsoever latitude they shall be that lie within the entrance of the straights commonly called Hudson's Straights together with all the lands and territories upon the countries, coasts, and confines of the seas, bays, lakes, rivers, creeks, and sounds aforesaid that are not already actually possessed by or granted to any of our subjects or possessed by the subjects of any other Christian prince or state.[1]

It is true that Canada had accepted the Company's ownership rights only reluctantly and after years of protest, putting forward the different theory that most of Rupert's Land ought to belong to Canada because of the explorations undertaken from New France. But the Colonial Office refused any measures that might diminish the Company's rights, and in the end the sale went through on the assumption that the Company was the rightful owner of this immense territory.

When the *Métis* of Red River, who had never been consulted about the sale, showed signs of resistance, the Canadian government refused to take possession, much as a purchaser might refuse to take possession of a house which had undergone damage in the period between signing of contract and date of transfer. The Imperial government doubted the legality of Canada's position but did not force the issue. Canada invited the inhabitants of Red River to send a delegation to Ottawa to make their concerns known. Having discussed matters with the three delegates (Father N.-J. Ritchot, Alfred Scott, John Black), the Canadian government drafted the Manitoba Act to respond to the desires of Red River: provincial status, responsible government, official bilingualism, protection of customary land rights, etc. Importantly, the Manitoba Act was a unilateral action of the Canadian Parliament, not a treaty between independent partners (although it was probably *ultra vires* of the Canadian Parliament and had later to be confirmed by Imperial statute). Payment for Rupert's Land was made in London after the Company delivered the Deed of Surrender to the Colonial Office; and the Imperial government, by order-in-council of 23 June 1870, annexed Rupert's Land to Canada, effective 15 July.

It was always assumed by both governments that aboriginal rights of the Indians would be respected. Indeed section 14 of the order-in-council of 23 June 1870 specified that "any claims of Indians to compensation for lands required for purposes of settlement shall be disposed of by the Canadian Government in communication with the Imperial Government."[2] The *Métis* were not explicitly mentioned, but the Canadian government had already recognized their aboriginal rights in the Manitoba Act.

Native title was not seen as sovereignty in the European sense. Only a state could claim sovereignty, and the North American Indian tribes had never been organized as states. Hence the validity of claims to sovereignty made by European states on the basis of discovery, settlement, and conquest. Nor was Indian title understood as ownership in fee simple, for the nomadic tribes of North America had never marked off plots of land in a way compatible with European notions of private property. Indian title was interpreted as an encumbrance upon the underlying title to the land held by the sovereign. Indians had a real and enforceable right to support themselves on this land as they had from time immemorial. This right could be surrendered only to the sovereign, not to private parties; and compensation had to be paid for surrender, according to the ancient principle of common law that there should be no expropriation without compensation.

This understanding was legally articulated in the *St. Catherine's Milling Case,* decided by the Supreme Court of Canada in 1887 and the Judicial Committee of the Privy Council in 1889. There aboriginal title was defined in the context of a dispute between the governments of Ontario and Canada over who owned the lands ceded by the Ojibway in Treaty No. 3: the Crown in right of Canada or the Crown in right of Ontario? We can ignore this aspect of the dispute to concentrate on the issue of aboriginal title. To explain this concept, the judges resorted to the concept of usufruct, which in Roman law was the right to use and enjoy the fruits of property — usually slaves or a landed estate — without actually owning it. The holder of usufructuary rights could enjoy the property undisturbed during the life of those rights, but could not sell or otherwise alienate the property. At the expiration of the usufruct, the property reverted to the owner. The Canadian and British courts, seeking to interpret aboriginal title as it had developed over the centuries, used the concept of usufruct as an analogy. They cast the sovereign in the role of owner and the natives in the role of holders of "a personal and usufructuary right"[3] to occupy the land and support themselves from its produce. This limited right stemmed from the benevolence of the sovereign, who had not yet chosen to make use of the land in other ways. It was an internal concession made by the sovereign as part of Indian policy; it was not a right to be claimed under the law of nations by Indian tribes as if they were sovereign nations.

Title, thus, was vested in the Crown. The aboriginal right to use the land was an encumbrance on that title which had to be extinguished before the Crown could alienate the land to private owners. Extinguishment required compensation, which might take the form of land reserves, money payments, educational or medical services, etc. Logically, the situation was not different from other real estate conveyances where an encumbrance existed upon a title, as from mortgage or other debt. Title had to be cleared before alienation through sale or donation was possible.

The Canadian government acted on this basis to extinguish aboriginal rights in Rupert's Land. The Indians were dealt with in the numbered treaties of the 1870s, and a land grant of 1,400,000 acres was divided among the *Métis* of Manitoba. The only anomaly concerned the *Métis* of the North-West Territories, where delay had ensued for various reasons. But on the eve of the Rebellion, the government announced that it would also deal with them, although the precise form that compensation would take was apparently still undecided. This sequence of actions should have wiped the slate clean, according to the official view. All encumbrances to title should have been removed, all aboriginal rights extinguished. Without injustice to Indian or *Métis*, the government could open the land for homesteading, make land grants to railways or colonization companies, and in general act as a landlord with a clear title.

It is crucial to appreciate the intellectual framework within which the government acted. From offer to purchase through taking possession and finally clearing title, everything was based on the validity of the Hudson's Bay Company's charter and on the contemporary understanding of aboriginal rights. The quarrel with Riel arose in large part because he had a view of the situation which diverged at fundamental points. This view was never expressed completely and systematically, but it may be put together from various writings and utterances. Since many of these statements come from the months after the Rebellion was put down, there may be some question as to whether they adequately represent Riel's earlier ideas. We must presume they do; otherwise there is not enough material to analyze Riel's thinking at the pivotal moment of the Rebellion's outbreak. Apart from this one assumption, we will try not to impose an artificial consistency upon the thoughts of a man who was not a political philosopher.

Riel explicitly denied the validity of the Hudson's Bay charter because of its monopolistic provisions. The Company's sole right to trade "unjustly deprived the Northwest of the advantages of international trade and the rest of humanity, especially neighboring peoples, of the benefit of the commercial relations with the North-West to which they were entitled."[4] The result was impoverishment and oppression of the native inhabitants, both Indians and *Métis*. Riel coined the term *haute trahison internationale*[5] to describe the situation, which we might translate into today's idiom as "a crime against humanity." The charter was void, as was any sale based upon it; for the Company could not sell what it did not own. The most Riel would admit was that the Company had an interest in the land which it had sold to Canada;[6] but that transaction did not affect the natives, who were the true owners of the land. Aboriginal rights were clearly in Riel's mind not a mere encumbrance on the title but actual ownership — not individual ownership in fee simple, perhaps, but a collective ownership by the *Métis* as a nation and by the Indians as tribes. In effect, he reversed the official view according to which the

Hudson's Bay Company was the true owner of lands in which the natives possessed an interest consisting of the usufructuary right of subsistence. Riel made the natives the owners of lands in which the Company possessed the interest of being allowed to trade. They owned their land in the same way as all other nations owned their lands under the law of nations; their title was not merely a limited right of occupancy dependent on the grace of the sovereign. He stood in the tradition of *Métis* nationalism which stretched back to the conflict with the Hudson's Bay Company about the Selkirk Settlement. Traders of the Northwest Company had suggested to the *Métis* that the land was theirs, not the Company's, and the idea had persisted across the generations.

Riel had argued in a slightly different way when he established the Provisional Government on 8 December 1869. He issued a Declaration which somewhat grudgingly conceded the legitimacy of the Company's regime while remaining silent about the question of ownership:

> This Company consisting of many persons required a certain constitution. But as there was a question of commerce only their constitution was framed in reference thereto. Yet since there was at that time no government to see to the interests of a people already existing in the country, it became necessary for judicial affairs to have recourse to the officers of the Hudson's Bay Company. Thus inaugurated that species of government which, slightly modified by subsequent circumstances, ruled this country up to a recent date.

Although this government "was far from answering to the wants of the people," the *Métis* "had generously supported" it. But now the Company was abandoning its people by "subjugat[ing] it without its consent to a foreign power"; and according to the law of nations, a people abandoned by its government "is at liberty to establish any form of government it may consider suitable to its wants."[7] Thus the Provisional Government was legitimate according to the law of nations, and the Hudson's Bay Company had no right to transfer to Canada the land and people it had abandoned. Canada would have to deal with the Provisional Government if it was going to annex Rupert's Land.

Riel's original position of 1869 was that it violated that law of nations (or "international law" as we would say today) to transfer a population without seeking its consent. In 1885 he added the argument that the Company did not own Rupert's Land because its charter was void. Both arguments led to the same conclusions, that the sale to Canada was invalid until the inhabitants of Rupert's Land gave their consent, and that, living in a political vacuum, they certainly had the right to form their own government to negotiate the terms of sale on their behalf.

Riel not only sought to demonstrate the legitimacy of the Provisional Government through abstract reasoning, but also tried to show that the Provisional Government had been recognized by both Britain and Canada. He formulated the facts slightly differently on various occasions, but the main line of argument was always the same: ministers of the Canadian government had invited the insurgents to send delegates to Ottawa and had conducted negotiations with them. An amnesty had been promised by the governor general himself, both directly and through intermediaries. Thus both Canada and Britain had recognized the Provisional Government *de facto*, even if there had not been a formal exchange of ambassadors according to international protocol.[8]

The legitimacy of the Provisional Government was essential to Riel because it determined his interpretation of the Manitoba Act and of the entry of Manitoba into Confederation. His frame of reference was the law of nations (*droit des gens*), because negotiations had been carried out between independent entities, Canada and Red River. Rupert's Land had not been purchased; rather its inhabitants, acting through their government, had decided to join Canada. Union with Canada was not the result of unilateral action in Ottawa; it had required the assent of the Provisional Government, which was formally given after Father Ritchot returned from Ottawa to report on the terms offered by Canada. After the vote, Riel's "secretary of state" wrote to Canada's secretary of state to inform him that

> . . . the Provisional Government and the Legislative Assembly, in the name of the people of the North-West, do accept the "Manitoba Act," and consent to enter into Confederation on the terms entered into with our delegates. . . . The Provisional Government and the Legislative Assembly have consented to enter into Confederation in the belief, and on the understanding, that in the above mentioned terms a general amnesty is contemplated.[9]

The arrangement was a "treaty" in the sense of an international agreement between states. The treaty had two parts: the written text of the Manitoba Act and the oral promise of amnesty for all actions committed over the winter of 1869–70. This explains the final lines of Riel's pamphlet on the amnesty question:

> Ce que nous demandons, c'est l'amnistie: c'est l'exécution loyale

de l'acte de Manitoba. Rien de plus, mais aussi rien de moins. [What we demand is amnesty — the fulfillment in good faith of the Manitoba Act — nothing more, but also nothing less.][10]

Riel literally meant that the annexation of Rupert's Land was the result of a "solemn treaty"[11] which, like all treaties, would become void if it were not observed. Ergo the annexation was reversible. The people of Rupert's Land, which had become the Province of Manitoba and the North-West Territories, could remove themselves from Canada if the treaty was broken in either of its branches: the amnesty or the Manitoba Act.

In Riel's view, Canada had betrayed its obligations under both headings. We will not go into the amnesty question here. It was certainly never far from Riel's mind, but it would not have sufficed to raise the flag of revolt among the *Métis* in 1885. This purpose was served by Riel's interpretation of the Manitoba Act, particularly of section 31, which authorized the half-breed land grant. At its time of entry into Confederation, Manitoba consisted of approximately 9,500,000 acres. With the 1,400,000 acres set aside by section 31 for the "children of half breed heads of families," the government clearly thought to equip each young *Métis* with enough land to make him economically self-sufficient. It was the same principle as the one by which Indian reserves were calculated at the rate of a quarter-section of land per family of five. The government was thinking in terms of the future needs of a special group among the population.

Riel, on the contrary, viewed the 1,400,000 acres as the sale price of the 9,500,000 acres comprised in Manitoba. This ratio set a precedent for the rest of the land of the North-West. As subsequent acres were opened for settlement, the *Métis* of those areas should receive a similar price, in order to extinguish their aboriginal title, namely one-seventh of the land or the financial value of the one-seventh. This would amount to about 176,000,000 acres for the North-West outside the original boundaries of Manitoba.[12]

Riel's single best explanation of this theory was given in his final trial speech. It must be read carefully, for his phrasing in English is sometimes awkward, even though the ideas are clear and logically developed:

> But somebody will say, on what grounds do you ask one-seventh of the lands? In England, in France, the French and the English have lands, the first was in England, they were the owners of the soil and they transmitted to generations. Now, by the soil they have had their start as a nation. Who starts the nations? The very one who creates them, God. God is the master

of the universe, our planet is his land, and the nation and the tribes are members of His family, and as a good father, he gives a portion of his lands to that nation, to that tribe, to everyone, that is his heritage, that is his share of the inheritance, of the people, or nation or tribe. Now, here is a nation strong as it may be, it has its inheritance from God. When they have crowded their country because they had no room to stay anymore at home, it does not give them the right to come and take the share of all tribes besides them. When they come they ought to say, well, my little sister, the Cree tribe, you have a great territory, but that territory has been given to you as our own land, it has been given to our fathers in England or in France and of course you cannot exist without having that spot of land. This is the principle God cannot create a tribe without locating it. We are not birds. We have to walk on the ground, and that ground is encircled of many things, which besides its own value, increases its value in another manner, and when we cultivate it we still increase that value. Well, on what principle can it be that the Canadian Government have given one-seventh to the half-breeds of Manitoba? I say it must be on this ground, civilization has the means of improving life that Indians or half-breeds have not. So when they come in our savage country, in our uncultivated land, they come and help us with their civilization, but we helped them with our lands, so the question comes: Your land, you Cree or you half-breed, your land is worth to-day one-seventh of what it will be when the civilization will have opened it? Your country unopened is worth to you only one-seventh of what it will be when opened. I think it is a fair share to acknowledge the genius of civilization to such an extent as to give, when I have seven pair of socks, six, to keep one. They made the treaty with us. As they made the treaty, I say they have to observe it, and did they observe the treaty? No.[13]

The statement accepts and justifies the surrender of land by aboriginal peoples in return for compensation. To that extent, it is compatible with the official Indian policy of Britain and Canada. Beyond that, however, lie some marked differences. Riel seems to challenge the unilateral assumption of sovereignty which was the foundation of British rule in North America. (I say "seems to challenge" because his language is ambiguous; he does not distinguish between sovereignty and ownership). In any case, he certainly does not accept the principle of unilateral extinguishment of aboriginal title through legislation. The land grant of section 31 was valid compensation for surrender of land only inasmuch as it was part of a treaty approved by both sides. Furthermore, the basis of compensation was a *quid pro quo* as in any sale. Because the advantages of civilization could multiply the value of land seven times or more, the *Métis* would be at least as well off by surrendering six-sevenths of their land and adopting civilized ways while retaining one-seventh (or its money equivalent). It was most decidedly not a matter of government allocating a certain amount of land to each *Métis* individual. In another text, Riel derided this approach as a "sophism" designed to let the government "evade its obligations" and "frustrate the *Métis*, as a group or nationality, of their seventh of the lands."[14]

Riel's insistence on the principle of "the seventh" nicely illustrates the theoretical difference between his position and the official view. According to the latter, aboriginal title was only a "personal and usufructuary right" of the natives to gather subsistence from the land. If it was to be extinguished, it was logical to compute compensation on the basis of the number of persons who would now have to subsist in other ways. Riel, however, maintained that the natives were the true proprietors of the soil in the full sense of ownership. Thus compensation for expropriation should be based on the value of the land, not on the number of people affected. To use a modern analogy, if a provincial government has to expropriate land for, say, a hydroelectric transmission line, it would compensate owners according to the fair market value of the asset, not according to the size of their families. Riel's understanding of the nature of aboriginal title drove him to demand analogous treatment for the *Métis*.

The government grudgingly agreed to a new issue of scrip to provide for the relatively few *Métis* who had not participated in the Manitoba land grant. But in Riel's mind, the whole North-West outside Manitoba still belonged to the *Métis*. The Hudson's Bay Company had sold whatever interest it had, and the Indians, at least in the fertile belt, had signed land surrender treaties. It was still necessary to extinguish the *Métis* title, and that could not be done with a few pieces of scrip. It would require payment of the value of one-seventh of the whole North-West, following the precedent solemnly established in the "Manitoba Treaty." And if that treaty continued to be broken, the *Métis* would no longer be part of Canada. According to the law of nations, they could once again form a Provisional Government and undertake negotiations with other governments. There might be a new treaty with Canada, or perhaps the North-West would become a separate colony within the Empire, or perhaps it would even ask for annexation to the United States, as Riel did after his trial. Everything was possible. It is this train of thought, and only this, which makes the North-West Rebellion intelligible.

THE AGITATION

When Riel came to Saskatchewan on 1 July 1884, it was expected that his work would last only a brief time. The people knew what they wanted; all they needed from Riel was advice on the best way of pressing their demands within constitutional limits. But nothing was sent to the government until 16 December 1884, and that petition was only a preliminary draft. Work on further declarations continued well into February 1885. Why did things drag on for such a long time? Probably because Riel was trying to unite several incompatible points of view:

1) His own radical theory that the North-West Territories were free to leave Confederation if Canada continued to refuse large-scale compensation for extinguishment of *Métis* aboriginal rights.

2) The desire of the *Métis* for an issue of scrip and settlement of their disputes with the Department of the Interior. Their aims were moderate; but, as events would show, many of them were willing to resort to arms to achieve their goals.

3) The desire of the English half-breeds for the same goals as the *Métis*. The difference was that the half-breeds were not willing to take up arms.

4) The intention of a group of white businessmen in Prince Albert, mostly allied to the Liberal Party, to win provincial status and responsible government for the North-West. Their most active figure, William Henry Jackson, was willing to consider separation from Canada, but it is not known whether there was much support for his extreme position.

5) The demand of the more militant Indians, whose most prominent spokesman was Big Bear, for a renegotiation of treaties on more favorable terms.

Riel tried to coalesce all these groups around his own views, but irreconcilable differences made the coalition unstable. The *Métis* were willing to follow him, except for those, particularly of the merchant class, who disapproved of armed force. The English half-breeds could accept his demand for a massive settlement of aboriginal rights, but they also disapproved of force. William Henry Jackson and perhaps others among the whites were willing to consider a rupture with Canada, but they were put off by Riel's ideas on aboriginal rights, which would have enriched the *Métis*, half-breeds, and Indians at the expense of the white community.

In the nine months between his return to Canada and the outbreak of the Rebellion, Riel grappled with this political problem. He wrote or collaborated on the writing of several documents, but none was completed. Those which expressed his own views could not command universal support among the different groups, while those which could be supported did not express his own radical theory. Thus no single text was produced which adequately expressed all the demands which led to the Rebellion.

Let us now follow the course of the agitation from Riel's return to Canada up to the eve of the Rebellion. This is not a general history of these months, which has been well written by Stanley and others. It is a study of the intellectual difficulties faced by Riel in melding his own views with those of the groups he hoped to organize under his leadership. The analysis is sometimes speculative because very little written by Riel during the period of the agitation has been found. However, there is abundant material in the papers of Riel's collaborator, William Henry Jackson, with which to fill the gaps.[15]

Riel was received at Fish Creek on 1 July. He made public appearances to the *Métis* and half-breeds within the next two weeks, but we do not know what he said. His first major appearance was a speech in Prince Albert, 19 July. His own notes, and the various transcripts of the speech, show that he stressed provincial status and responsible government, themes dear to that audience. "Let the people of Assiniboia, of Alberta, of Saskatchewan petition in the proper manner for immediat[e] admission as provinces in the confederation." Riel also admonished his listeners to insist on provincial control of public lands, which had been denied Manitoba. But they were to strive for all this strictly "within the bonds of constitutional energy."[16] One account reports a brief reference to aboriginal rights;[17] but the reporter garbled what Riel said, and probably its full significance was not apparent to the audience.

Shortly after this meeting Jackson circulated an open letter to residents of Prince Albert and the surrounding area. It began: "We are starting a movement in this settlement with a view to attaining Provincial Legislatures for the North-West Territories and if possible the control of our own resources, that we may build our railroads and other works to aid our own interests rather than those of the Eastern Provinces." Readers were asked to send delegates to the executive committee, "which will be called together in a few days to put our own statement of rights in final shape." The petition would be sent to Ottawa for action by the Canadian government, though Jackson also mentioned a more radical option: "Possibly we may settle up with the East and form a separate Federation of our own in direct connection with the crown." There was no mention of the *Métis*, except to say that Riel had united them "solidly in our favour"; nor was there mention of Riel's special theories.[18]

Jackson's reference to "a few days" shows he was thinking of quick action. This is confirmed by a letter he wrote to Riel the same day: "Today I shall finish up work in town and tomorrow start for the Lower Flat etc. I will try and get out to your place toward end of week. Please be working up the petition into shape and we will get it in neat form before the committee is called to endorse or alter it."[19] This sense of urgency was apparently shared by Riel, for he wrote at this time that he intended to return to Montana around September.

The petition which Jackson expected to finish in a few days has been preserved among his papers. It chided the British government for having permitted the North-West Territories to be governed by men "chosen by and responsible to not the people of the said Territories but the people of the Eastern Provinces."[20] A long list of grievances mentioned public works and services, taxation, tariffs, monopolies, and other topics of interest to local businessmen. Homestead regulations got only a few lines, and aboriginal rights were barely mentioned. It was clearly a Prince Albert document, one that would have little appeal to the Métis or to Riel, except that he would have been in accord with its closing demand that the Territories "be forthwith formed into Provinces, each Province having full control of its own resources and internal administration, and having power to send a just number of representatives to the Federal legislature."[21]

Another and much more radical draft seems to be connected with Jackson's idea of "settling up with the East." Alleging that the "Government of Eastern Canada hath grossly exceeded and abused" its trusteeship over the North-West, it calls upon Great Britain

> to assert its suspended Guardianship and remove the Trustee-
> ship of the said lands from the hands of the Gov't of Eastern
> Canada and place it in the hands of a council composed partly of
> members elected by the actual residents to protect interests of
> actual settlers, and partly of members nominated by Brit. Gov't.
> to protect interests of future settlers.[22]

August brought two reasons for delay. When a visit from Minister of Public Works Sir Hector Langevin was announced, it was decided to present a list of grievances to him; but he cancelled his trip late in the month. The second reason for delay was a broadening of the movement to include the Indians. In the first ten days of August there was a council of several Cree bands at the Duck Lake reserve. Several speakers denounced the treaties and called for renegotiation. Jackson seems to have been present and taken notes, for the speeches are recorded in his hand. Riel apparently did not attend, but he was in contact with the chiefs through intermediaries. Later in August Riel and Big Bear met at Jackson's house in Prince Albert.[23] These delays caused resentment among the English half-breeds. James Isbister wrote to Riel on 4 September: "I cannot for a moment, understand what is your delay, in not having our Committee meeting, sitting and working. . . . I must say we the people of the Ridge, Red Deer Hill, Halcro's Settlement, and St. Catherine Parish find you are too slow, or does the delay rest with W. Jackson and his people?"[24] Isbister, one of those who had gone to Montana to fetch Riel, had been the earliest farmer around Prince Albert, and his opinion carried great weight. But even as Riel received this letter, he was off on another tack, this time particularly concerned with the Métis.

On 5 September the Métis held a large meeting at St. Laurent to discuss their grievances with Bishop Grandin, who was making a pastoral visit. Riel read aloud a memorandum of eleven points. Two days later, as Grandin left for Regina, Riel gave him a slightly abridged written version containing eight items.

It is not clear why the list was reduced from eleven to eight. Perhaps it was only because Riel was writing in haste under awkward conditions. One of the three omitted points was a demand for better rations for the Indians. Riel, complaining that the Métis and other settlers were forced to support the Indians, had called on the government to "make the Indians work as Pharaoh had made the Jews work" — a proposal that may lift some eyebrows among those who now regard him as a humanitarian. A second point was a request that the government should pay a thousand dollars to build a convent wherever there were enough Métis to justify the nuns in coming to found a school. The third point was a demand for provincial status for the districts of the North-West as soon as their populations equalled that of Manitoba in 1870. Provincial status "should be accompanied by all the advantages of responsible government, including the administration of public lands."[25] The first two of the omitted points were rather peripheral to the agitation and to Riel's long-term goals, but the third was absolutely fundamental, so its omission is curious.

Its main idea was, however, partially included in the first item of the eight-point list given to Grandin, which called for "the inauguration of responsible government." Four other points on the list covered long-standing grievances of the local Métis. Riel wanted "the same guarantees . . . as those accorded to the old settlers of Manitoba," which implied several things such as river lots, hay and wood privilege, and squatter's rights. He demanded patents for the plots of land along the Saskatchewan on which the Métis had settled, often in disregard of homestead rules. A land grant similar to that in Manitoba would of course be required. Finally Riel requested that more contracts for public works be let to local inhabitants. These were all old items of complaint, and Riel's document added nothing new to their formulation.

The list did, however, contain three points, stemming directly from Riel, which added a whole new dimension to the Métis demands.

> 5. That two million acres be set apart by the government for the benefit of the half breeds, both Protestant and Catholic. That the government sell these lands; that it deposit the money in the bank, and that the interest on that money serve for the support of schools, for the construction of orphanages and hospitals, for the support of institutions of this type already constructed, and to obtain carts for poor half breeds as well as seed for the annual spring planting.
>
> 6. That a hundred townships, selected from swampy lands which do not appear habitable at the moment, be set aside by the government and that every eighteen years there take place a distribution of these lands to the half breed children of the new generation. This to last 120 years.
>
> 7. The Province of Manitoba has been enlarged since 1870. The half breed title to the lands by which it was enlarged has not yet been extinguished. Let that title be extinguished in favour of the half breed children born in the province since the transfer [i.e. since 15 July 1870] and in favour of the children born there for the next four generations.[26]

Item 5 amounted to a Métis trust fund designed to promote their economic and social advancement, while item 6 would have insured the availability of land to several new generations of Métis. Item 7, although vague, had the most radical implications, for it hinted at Riel's theory that Métis ownership rights to the North-West were still alive. All these points flow from his idea of collective ownership of the North-West by the Métis nation. Riel was asking for a two million acre reserve, plus a hundred townships (2,304,000 acres), plus something for the expansion of Manitoba: a considerable amount in all, but far less than one-seventh of the North-West. These demands were moderate because they were only a first instalment, as shown by Riel's postscript to the document: "This is what we ask while we wait for Canada to become able to pay us the annual interest on the sum that our land is worth and while we wait for public opinion to agree to recognize our rights to the land in their fullest extent (dans toute leur étendue)."[27] Grandin gave a copy of Riel's text to Governor Dewdney, who forwarded an English translation to Sir John A. Macdonald. The bishop stated that he supported the traditional demands of the Métis but that he could not speak to the political questions of responsible government and aboriginal title.[28] Macdonald received additional information about Riel's postscript from A.-E. Forget, who had accompanied Grandin. Forget reported that Riel's document

> only purports to contain such requests as need an immediate settlement. In addition to these advantages, they claim that their right to land can only be fully extinguished by the annual payment of the interest on a capital representing the value of land in the Territories estimated to be worth at the time of transfer twenty-five cents an acre for the halfbreeds and fifteen cents for the Indians. This is the claim alluded to in the post-scriptum of Riel's memo to His Lordship.[29]

Forget added that the *Métis* were planning to draw up a memorial on this basis and send it to the House of Commons. He tried to persuade them to direct it to the governor general in council through Governor Dewdney.

A draft of such a memorial exists in Riel's hand, addressed to "Your Excellency in Council." The heading suggests it was written out after the conversation with Forget on 7 September, although earlier drafts must have preceded this neatly written text. Unaccountably long overlooked, this document is an invaluable statement of Riel's true objectives.[30]

The text began by denouncing the Indian treaties as a swindle because they "are not based on a reasonable estimation of the value of their lands." The Indians would not be content until they receive this value. "It is the opinion of your humble petitioners that the land in its uncultivated state, with its natural wealth of game, fish, and berries cannot be worth less to the Indian than twelve and a half cents per acre." The same principle applied to the *Métis*, except that the land was worth twenty-five cents an acre to them because their usage of it was "fairly civilized." Then followed some calculations, based on certain assumptions:

— 1,100,000,000 acres of land in the North-West
— 100,000 Indians
— 100,000 *Métis*
— 5% interest rate

The result of these assumptions was an annuity of $68.75 for each Indian and $137.50 for each *Métis*. However, not too much importance was attached to these calculations, which were "only approximate." They were offered only to give "a fair idea" of *Métis* rights and to suggest "the profound distress in which the Dominion of Canada plunges us by taking possession of our lands and not giving us the adequate compensation we expect of it."[31]

The line of reasoning embodied in this petition was not a temporary aberration on Riel's part. He reproduced exactly the same argument in his last major piece of writing, published posthumously as "Les Métis du Nord-Ouest," except that he used figures of fifteen cents an acre for the Indians and thirty cents an acre for the Métis.[32] Furthermore, the total amounts of money involved were of the same magnitude as the value of the one-seventh of the North-West demanded at the trial.[33] The notion of a trust fund based on the value of the land surrendered flowed directly from Riel's conception of aboriginal title as collective ownership, not a mere encumbrance on the sovereign's title, and was in direct contrast to the official policy of calculating compensation proportionally to numbers of individuals rather than to the area of land involved.

Why this petition dropped completely from sight is one of the riddles of the agitation. One may conjecture that its radical theory of aboriginal rights was unacceptable to the white settlers whose support was indispensable to a joint movement. Collaboration with the white settlers and English half-breeds became very active in September. An important meeting was held 10 September at the home of Andrew Spence of Red Deer Hill. A brief minute of that meeting in the hand of Jackson shows the internal strains to which the movement was subject: "Committee met at Red Deer Hill, Andrew Spence's residence Wednesday afternoon, dispute whether Bill of Rights or petition. Committee appointed to prepare samples of both."[34]

As will be shown below, the "petition" was to be a list of grievances submitted to the government for redress. Compiling such a document was a purely constitutional action. The "Bill of Rights" was to be a more sweeping statement of the right of the people of the North-West to self-determination. To speak in such terms would at least be to border on sedition, and the committee was still undecided whether to go that far.

Not surprisingly, it was easier to compile the petition than the Bill of Rights. A draft seems to have been completed as early as 22 September,[35] and two days later a copy was sent to Archbishop Taché.[36] Further copies were mailed on 1 October to Father Constantine Scollen, an Oblate missionary in Alberta, and to J. W. Taylor, American Consul in Winnipeg.[37]

Of the three copies sent out, the only one to have been found is Taylor's. Written entirely in Riel's hand, it is very little different from the later draft sent to the secretary of state on 16 December. It was mostly concerned with the redress of specific grievances without challenging the government's authority. But the final paragraph showed a larger strategy:

> Your humble petitioners are of opinion that the shortest and most effectual methods of remedying these grievances would be to grant the N.W.T. responsible government with control of its own resources [sic] and just representation in the federal Parliament and Cabinet. Wherefor[e] your petitioners humbly pray that your excellency in council would be pleased to cause the introduction, at the coming session of Parliament, of a measure providing for the complete organization of the District of Saskatchewan as a province; and that they be allowed, as in 70, to send delegates to Ottawa with their Bill of Rights, whereby an understanding may be arrived at as to their entry into confederation with the constitution of a free Province.[38]

The dispute over whether to prepare a petition or a Bill of Rights had been resolved by deciding to submit the petition first, followed by a Bill of Rights.

The document's meaning is not fully apparent until one recalls Riel's interpretation of the events of 1870. He was not merely calling for the government to hear and act upon complaints; he was proposing a new "treaty" in the international framework of the law of nations. This analysis is confirmed by Riel's covering letter to Taylor, which made the point emphatically:

> The people of the Northwest are poor. They are not happy under the Canadian rule; not only because their public affairs are improperly administered by the federal government, but because they are practically denied by that government the enjoyment *of the right of people.* [Riel's emphasis] That is principally what is ruining them.[39]

Another mystery of the agitaton is that nothing further happened for two and a half months after this burst of activity in September. It may be that Riel and the others were waiting for signatures to be gathered. We know little about this, but efforts to obtain signatures in other parts of the Territories seem to have been made.[40] It may also be that they were waiting for reactions to the copies they had sent out.

Taché's reply was not slow in coming, nor was it encouraging. He told Riel to "give up useless agitation, give up certain ambiguities of language whose true meaning would not escape those who reflect."[41] He had obviously divined the implications of allusions to a Bill of Rights. Father Scollen, less politically sophisticated, was more positive. He passed the petition on to Dan Maloney, a political figure of St. Albert who had befriended the Métis on other occasions. Maloney promised to do what he could to intercede with the government on their behalf.[42]

The final version of the petition, hardly changed from the text of late September, was sent on 16 December to the secretary of state. There were several odd things about the submission which could not but detract from the impression it made in Ottawa. Although the petition was written out in longhand by Riel, his name did not appear anywhere. The petition in fact is unsigned, although earlier researchers, confusing the petition with the covering letter, have claimed it bore the names of W. H. Jackson and Andrew Spence.[43] There certainly is no long list of signatures of the kind one would expect to accompany such a petition. It seems that this submission was only preliminary, for Jackson was occupied after the New Year in collecting signatures. Apparently he intended to resubmit the signed petition directly to the governor general. A covering letter, rather bold in tone, was provided by Jackson, who signed himself "Secretary General Committee," without explaining the nature of the committee:

> the petition is an extremely moderate one. . . . to the Canadian and English wing of the movement a more searching exposition of the situation would have been much more satisfactory. The opinion has been freely expressed that our appeal should be directed to the Privy Council of England and to the general public rather than to the federal authorities.[44]

Jackson's choice of words was deliberately disingenuous. He admitted elsewhere that the petition "was purposely made weak, as a blind," because the agitators were not yet ready to show their hand to the government.[45] The petition gave the impression that it was one last attempt at moderation, which might be followed by more extreme measures if concessions were not made immediately; yet Jackson and Riel were already preparing their next steps even before the petition could have reached its target. On 18 December, Jackson, back in Prince Albert, wrote to Riel that he would be down to see him in ten days or so, adding, "In the meantime please work away at your proclamation," probably a reference to the Bill of Rights.[46]

It cannot be emphasized too strongly that this petition was only secondarily an appeal to the Canadian government for redress of grievances, although it has generally been presented that way in the historical literature. It was primarily a step in a bigger campaign whose objectives, although not absolutely certain, were on a grand scale. Immediate provincial status, control of natural resources, renegotiation of the terms of Confederation, separation from Canada, and a vast settlement of aboriginal claims were all possible outcomes. The concrete grievances of the Métis had become merely a means to these ends.

The petition's ulterior purpose helps explain its peculiar structure. It was divided into two parts of roughly equal size: sixteen particular items of complaint, followed by a seventeenth item of great length rehearsing the events of 1870 and the government's subsequent failure to observe the "treaty." The sixteen points corresponded to specific grievances; the seventeenth laid the foundation of a demand for self-determination under the law of nations.

The specific grievances fell into several categories. One demand called for better rations for the Indians. Another called for a half-breed land grant as in Manitoba. Eight items concerned the complicated issues of survey and homestead requirements. The remaining six are readily identifiable as standard tenets of western Liberalism: greater efficiency and economy in public works and buildings, a Hudson's Bay railway, strict liquor laws, secret ballot, and free trade. This part of the petition was truly a comprehensive, if miscellaneous, catalog of local dissatisfactions.

The seventeenth point was in contrast a long, tightly reasoned chain of argument: the people of the North-West in 1870 had sent representatives to Ottawa who were recognized "as the Delegates of the North-West." Even as Canada negotiated with them, she was preparing a military expedition. Promises of amnesty were made and not fulfilled. The Imperial order-in-council annexing Rupert's Land to Canada was passed before the people of the North-West had a chance to ratify the agreement. Since that time Canada had continued to violate the "treaty" by denying provincial status to the North-West, by excluding Westerners from the cabinet, and by retaining control of natural resources. Riel did not openly state the conclusion of the argument, namely that the broken "treaty" had released the people of the North-West from allegiance to Canada, but he hinted at it obliquely, stating that inhabitants of the North-West "are treated neither according to their privileges as British subjects nor according to the rights of people." The implication is clear to anyone familiar with Riel's thinking. The petition closed with virtually the same words as those of the draft of October, calling for delegates to take a Bill of Rights to Ottawa and negotiate entry into Confederation.

Not much came of this petition. A formal acknowledgment was sent to Jackson, while the document was sent to William Pearce for comment. In a point-by-point analysis, he argued that the specific grievances were based on misconceptions or were being dealt with.[47] Indeed the government had already made an inquiry into the homestead problems of St. Laurent and had decided to do something about scrip. Ironically, the petition had arrived after the major problems of the *Métis* were on the way to resolution.

However, the long-range plans of Riel and Jackson were very much alive, as we may deduce from a letter of 27 January. Having received a formal acknowledgment of the petition, Jackson wrote:

> I think with you [Riel] that the mere fact of an answer is a very good sign considering the bold tone of my letter and our audacious assumption that we are not yet in Confederation, an assumption which it seems to me, they have conceded in their letter.[48]

This was surely building on air, for the acknowledgment had only stated that "the matter will receive due consideration." But Jackson was looking for favorable signs for his work. His letter spoke rather confusingly of several documents he had drawn up. There was a reference to a petition for which he was collecting signatures, probably the petition which had already been submitted without signatures to the secretary of state. He may have planned to get it signed and resubmit it with more publicity. Also mentioned were

> a memorial suitable to catch the [Parliamentary] opposition in case the Council [i.e. cabinet] pay no attention — a stronger memorial for the Imperial sec'y of state for the Colonies in case the Federal Parliament pays no attention — and the Declaration of Rights for private circulation, and use if necessary. I will get all these documents signed along with the petition.[49]

The order of the documents suggests a strategy of appeals to cabinet, Parliament, and Great Britain, followed by a unilateral declaration of independence, if necessary. Jackson anticipated quick action as the parliamentary session was about to open, but he was also prepared for delays: "I will have the councillors in good heart for an unlimited period of quietness if found unavoidable. They must learn that quietness does not necessarily mean stagnation."

The description of the strategy was amplified in an undated note by Jackson. The plan was

> to organize every settlement & the N.W.T. convene a central congress in about two months and take our case direct to the throne. In the meantime we will send down a softly worded petition which will leave them under the impression that if they remove some of our present grievances, we will cease to agitate

for the power to prevent other grievances. They will therefore ease the present situation by giving us a greater share of grain contract and an order to float cash among us, and we will then have the sinews of war to go for stronger measures. The Bill of Rights is composed so as to cover the whole North West. The various examples of the resolution of those rights will be collected in each settlement, and we will then have a clear case for the Privy Council.[50]

And more radical still:

Platform

1. In regard to Government:
   Petition Brit. Govt. to appoint Commit. & transfer Govt. to council.
       In case of refusal declare Independence and appoint Council & assume control.[51]

The most interesting document to recover would be the Bill of Rights, but it was deliberately burnt shortly before the battle of Duck Lake.[52] No one has stated why it was destroyed, but perhaps Riel felt it to be incriminating. His explanation of the revolt was that the *Métis* had taken up arms in self-defense, fearing they were about to be attacked by the Mounted Police.[53] That theory would have been seriously compromised by a Bill of Rights showing that an uprising had long been posited as a possible last step if other measures failed.

Some idea of the Bill of Rights can be gleaned from Jackson's letter of 27 January. As the Bill was an English document, Riel had left the writing to Jackson, who had looked up precedents in law books; but the thought came from Riel. His central principle was that "the world is governed by justice." It was unjust "that the inhabitants of any section of the Globe should possess the right of irresponsible and infallible authority over the inhabitants of some other section of the Globe." Such rule from afar would despoil its subjects, subjecting them to injustice. The aboriginal inhabitants had self-government, and this "consistency between their institutions and natural law . . . resulted in fair play & prosperity to each member of the community." But the introduction by the colonial powers of "irresponsible authority" had led to general misery. The declaration concluded "with the assertion of the natural right of self-government thus proven." It was obviously meant not as a theoretical statement but a call to action; Jackson was putting it "into such a simple shape that any ordinary man could catch the main drift of the argument at first reading."[54]

Although Riel and Jackson seemed agreed on strategy, signs of strain were already beginning to show in their alliance. A bizarre episode took place on 14 or 15 January when Riel was having dinner at the Jackson home in Prince Albert. He was served an end cut of roast beef, rather heavily seasoned with salt and pepper. After he tasted it, he ran outside and made himself vomit. Then he went to Father André's residence to fetch Charles Nolin, whom he mysteriously informed that attempts were being made to poison him. The incident, improbable as it sounds, is attested in several independent sources.[55] A few days later, Jackson wrote to the Edmonton newspaperman Frank Oliver: "Efforts are being made to separate Riel and myself, but though we differ on certain theoretical points we have too much confidence in each other's honesty of purpose for such attempts to succeed."[56]

In the first two weeks of February Jackson made the round of the English settlements, collecting signatures for the petition, memorials, and Bill of Rights. According to one report, he also had people sign an authorization for him to be their delegate to Canada.[57] On 14 February, he went upriver to the French parishes to collect more signatures. It was on this trip that he and Riel came into open conflict. According to the subsequent account of T. Eastwood Jackson, William's brother, "[Riel] opposed the petition, attacking it on the basis of Halfbreed ownership, and my brother being equally determined on the other side, the argument lasted all night, and became so fierce that Riel lost his self-control."[58] If Eastwood may be believed, William was kept under house arrest, from which he twice tried unsuccessfully to escape. Whatever the precise details, it was definitely the end of the collaboration between Riel and Jackson as equal partners.

After the Rebellion was over and Jackson had been sent to a lunatic asylum, he briefly explained what had caused the argument. He had maintained his conviction

> that the particles of matter composing the Earth were the property of whosoever first chose to develop them into articles of utility except in case of the express allocation of land as in the case of Canaan, while Mr. Riel was, if I remember, pursuing the argument which I see he advanced on the occasion of his trial of Regina — that *every* nation is allotted its means of existence in the shape of a *land*.[59]

Since it hinges on the idea of uniting one's labor to the land to form property, Jackson's view may loosely be called Lockean. His report of his opinions corresponds substantially to a letter he wrote on 2

February 1885 to Albert Monkman, a leader of the agitation who moved in both the *Métis* and English half-breed communities.

> Let this be our aim. Let us sink all distinctions of race and religion. Let the white man delight in seeing the Indian helped forward to fill his place as a producer of wealth, and let the Indian and Halfbreed scorn to charge a rent for the soil which God has given to man, upon the settler who comes in to help to build up the country. . . . and let both unite in seeing that the fur country be managed for the benefit of the Indians who live by hunting, not for the good of a grasping company. Direct the attention of the Indian to the H.B.Co. monopoly, and to the necessity of providing schools for those who wish to learn productive arts, and turn them aside from the idea of being landlords. Why should God give a whole continent to 40,000 Indians and coop up 40,000,000 Englishmen in on a little island? The Indians are the same race; they, too, once lived in Europe. America was once without a man in it, why should a part of the human race go into that empty continent, and as soon as they have got there, turn round and forbid any more to come in, unless they pay for the privilege?[60]

It is not hard to see why Riel would have been enraged by such a cogent critique of the very idea of aboriginal title. It contradicted the basis of the agitation as he saw it. The agreement between Jackson and Riel on provincial status and responsible government was superficial compared to this profound disagreement about who really owned the North-West.

Riel began to assume a belligerent stance in public from 24 February onwards. Did the recent break with Jackson help steer him in that direction? Perhaps it made him feel that, if he continued the collaboration with the English, he would never be able to make his theory of aboriginal rights prevail.

Absence of documents, particularly on Riel's side, makes it likely that much will always remain obscure about the North-West agitation. But we know enough to realize how false is the naive version of events so often found in the contemporary literature. It would be more nearly true to tell the story thus: Riel saw in the grievances of the *Métis* an opportunity to implement his theory that the Manitoba "treaty" had been broken; that the *Métis* were the real owners of the North-West; that they could renegotiate entry into Confederation; that they must receive a seventh of the value of the land of the North-West as compensation for letting others live there; and that they could seek an independent political destiny if these terms were not met. Collaborating with white agitators like Jackson who were chiefly interested in provincial status and responsible government, he embarked upon a complex and deliberately deceptive strategy of making successively more radical demands. A Bill of Rights amounting to a Declaration of Independence was envisioned almost from the beginning. Finally, when Riel realized there was an unbridgeable gap between himself and Jackson, he determined to go it alone, as he had in 1869. The *Métis* would take the lead, rise in arms, and carry the English half-breeds and white settlers with them.

CHAPTER FIVE

RIEL'S PERSONAL INDEMNITY

One of the most intriguing questions about the origins of the North-West Rebellion is whether Riel made an attempt in the winter of 1884-85 to get for himself a large sum of money from the Canadian government. Allegedly, he promised to leave the North-West Territories and to persuade the *Métis* to be reconciled with the government if the latter would pay him $35,000 as first instalment on an indemnity which was eventually to total $100,000. Evidence in this direction was introduced at his trial through the testimony of Charles Nolin and Father André. No effective cross-examination on the subject was put up by the defense counsel, who were intent on demonstrating Riel's insanity. Nor did Riel himself deny that he had tried to get an indemnity from the government. He more or less admitted it in his final speech to the jury, and tried to show that the money was deserved.

Historians, clearly embarrassed by the episode, have tried to slide over it. Joseph Kinsey Howard gives it only one short paragraph, in which Father André seeks the money for Riel, who is not directly involved. George Woodcock gives it a slightly longer paragraph, but speculates that Riel may have only been playing games and asking for so much money "precisely because he did not intend to go." Howard Adams goes into the affair at some length, but transforms it into an offer from Macdonald, conveyed by André, to bribe Riel. The most complete and well-documented account in print is in George Stanley's biography *Louis Riel*, where the events are clearly sketched out. Yet Stanley leaves the impression that the whole business was the result of André's initiative. That impression is even stronger and clearer in the work of Stanley's youth, *The Birth of Western Canada*, which is much

more widely read than *Louis Riel.* Donald Creighton is the only major
writer to have interpreted Riel's attempt to get money as a true blot on
the man's character; and Creighton's opinion on a question like this
has been suspect to many because of his open partisanship for Sir
John A. Macdonald.[1] Thus it is not surprising that the episode is
ignored or understated in today's books of general Canadian history,
and that the Rebellion is commonly interpreted as a result of
governmental failure and Riel's idealism, rather than of his self-seek-
ing venality.

Obviously, it is important to have the truth. This chapter is a
reconstruction of the affair, based on all known sources.

An interview with Riel's cousin, Napoléon Nault, conducted in
1927 by the Comité Historique de L'Union Nationale Métisse
Saint-Joseph de Manitoba, diverges widely from all other accounts.
According to Nault:

> December 12, 1884, Riel said to me "Father André wants me
> to ask you to come with me." I went along. When we got there,
> after a moment of conversation, Father André asked Riel if he
> had been payed by the federal government for services rendered
> in Manitoba in 1869-70-71. Riel replied: "My only reward was
> five years of exile and a price on my head of five thousand
> dollars!" Father André said: "But you know the government
> owes you a tremendous amount! What would you say if I could
> get it for you?" "I doubt it very much," replied Riel, "but you
> can try anyway, if you wish."
>
> After leaving that interview, Riel called together his council
> and related the conversation he had just had. He expressed the
> hope that if Father André could obtain that indemnity, the best
> thing to do with it would be to found a newspaper which would
> be a powerful means of publicizing to the whole world the
> claims of his people. We talked at length about the figure to ask.
> Charles Nolin thought $100,000, but finally we agreed to settle
> for $35,000, the sum which was thought necessary to purchase a
> printing press and all the equipment to start a newspaper. Riel
> enquired during the following days where he could buy such
> things. He was thinking about it when he next met Father André
> on December 23. He spoke to him about it and explained his
> project. Father André said to him: "But then the question will be
> the same." "Father," said Riel, "doesn't the government owe me
> this money? You're the one who told me so. As to the *Métis*
> question, it won't be the same, for that money will furnish us a
> means which will greatly help us to improve our situation." Riel

recounted this second interview to his council, but we heard nothing further about it.[2]

If Nault's statement is reliable, Riel did not try to sell himself; others tried to buy him. Although researchers have been rather hesitant to accept Nault's account[3] it has undoubtedly contributed to creating the general impression found in the historical literature that the whole affair was a result of André's initiative, not Riel's.

In fact, there are strong reasons to be skeptical about Nault's story. For one thing, it was told in 1927, forty-two years after the events. Confusion of memory is obvious in Nault's reference to Riel's "council," for no council had yet been created in December 1884. For another, the story came from a cousin of Riel, who participated in the Rebellion and fled to the United States to escape prosecution; and it was printed by men who were intentionally trying to give a *Métis* version of history. Most importantly, Nault's account is contradicted by all contemporary documents. In such circumstances, to rely on Nault would violate all historical rules of evidence.

Louis Riel was a poor man. He had no family fortune to draw on, and his years of political involvement had left him little time to earn a living. For much of his adult life, he existed on the largesse of friends and relatives. He became self-supporting after he went to Montana in 1879, but he did not earn much money either as a petty trader dealing with the Indians or a school teacher at St. Peter's mission on the Sun River. When he did get money, he would use it up quickly, as in his quixotic lawsuit to stop the liquor traffic among the Montana *Métis*, or as in his large donation in 1883 to a religious order of nuns in St. Hyacinthe, Quebec.[4]

It is clear from his personal papers that Riel was at least a thousand dollars in debt when he left Montana in June 1884 to come to Saskatchewan.[5] He took pride in his poverty as a visible sign of his devotion to the *Métis* people, but it also preyed on his mind. He worried that he could not properly support his wife and two children. Furthermore, he blamed his penury on the Canadian government, as came out clearly in the speech at his trial where he explained why he had sought an indemnity from the government. In his view, he had performed a whole series of services for Canada which had been rewarded with unjust and harmful repression.

Riel's final trial speech included a veritable litany of grievances.[6] When the negotiations over the entry of Manitoba into Confederation had been completed in May 1870, G.-E. Cartier had said to Father Ritchot, "Let Mr. Riel continue to maintain order and govern the country, as he has done up to the present moment."[7] Riel did so until he was forced to flee before Colonel Wolseley's expeditionary force.

Not only was he never paid as governor of Red River, but also he was put to great expense in his flight. In 1871 he threw his influence against the Fenian raiders, but he received nothing more than a handshake from Governor Archibald. In 1872, he resigned his nomination in the riding of Provencher so that Cartier, defeated in Montreal East, could have a parliamentary seat; but the amnesty which Riel thought had been promised never came. He was elected three times to the House of Commons but could never take his seat because a reward for his capture offered by the government of Ontario made it unsafe for him to come to Ottawa. Instead, he was twice expelled by the House, and finally amnestied in 1875 only on condition of five years' banishment. This in turn meant he could not be in Manitoba in the late 1870s to receive his allotment when the half-breed land grant was distributed.

Riel also felt that the government of Canada had already acknowledged the justice of his claims to reparation for these injuries. It is well known that in December of 1871, Sir John A. Macdonald sent Archbishop Taché $5,000 to be given to Riel and Ambroise Lépine to persuade them to leave the country for a year. Riel and Lépine took the money after it had been supplemented by $3,000 from Donald A. Smith, then M.P. for Selkirk. They went to Minnesota in February 1872, though they returned to Manitoba after about four months, instead of staying away for a year, as had been expected. Riel also maintained that other offers had been made to him. In October 1873, when he was hiding in the woods to escape arrest, Father J. B. Proulx, on behalf of Macdonald, allegedly offered him $35,000 if he would leave the country for three years. When Alexander Mackenzie came to power, he also is supposed to have offered Riel a settlement through Father Lacombe in January 1874, and through two members of Parliament, Romuald Fiset and Alphonse Desjardins, in April. Nothing is known about these offers except what Riel said,[8] but there is probably some truth in his statements, for Riel had an excellent memory for names, places, and dates. He rejected these offers, whatever exactly they were; but in later years he may have sometimes wished that he had taken the money. His incorruptibility had earned him only exile from Canada and obscure poverty in the United States.

Against this background, it is easy to understand Riel's reaction when Gabriel Dumont, James Isbister, Moïse Ouellette, and Michel Dumas arrived at St. Peter's on 4 June 1884. They had been sent by the settlers of the Saskatchewan Valley to consult him about their political difficulties. Riel jumped at the chance to return to Canada, even though that was only one option presented by the delegates. When he wrote his formal reply to them, he made no secret that he was coming

to pursue his own claims as much as to help the people of the
Saskatchewan District:

> To be franc is the shortest. I doubt whether my advice given
> to you on this soil concerning affairs on canadian Territory
> could cross the borders and retain any influence. But here is
> another view. The Canadian Government owe me two hundred
> and forty acres of land according to the thirty-first clause of the
> Manitoba Treaty. They owe me also five lots, valuable on
> account of hay, timber & river frontage. Those lots were mine
> according to the different paragraphs of the same Thirty-first
> clause of the above mentioned Manitoba Treaty. It is the
> Canadian Government which have deprived me, directly or
> indirectly, of those properties. Besides, if they only pay attention
> to it a minute, they will easily find out that they owe me
> something else.
>
> Those my claims against them are such as to hold good,
> notwithstanding the fact that I have become American citizen.
> Considering then your interest and mine I accept your very kind
> invitation. I will go and spend some time amongst you. By
> petitioning the Government with you perhaps we will all have
> the good fortune of obtaining something. But my intention is to
> come back early this fall.[9]

The "two hundred and forty acres" to which Riel referred constituted
his share of the Manitoba half-breed land grant, in which he did not
participate. The reference to "five lots" is obscure; perhaps Riel had
staked certain claims in the Red River colony which were not
recognized later on. The "something else" mentioned by Riel
presumably included all the grievances he poured out in his trial
speech. This letter was read aloud when Riel was officially received by
the *Métis*, and a French translation was published the same month in
Le Manitoba.[10]

Money obviously remained on Riel's mind after his arrival in
Saskatchewan. In late July he wrote to his family in Manitoba:

> Not long ago I was a humble school teacher on the distant
> banks of the Missouri. And look at me today — one of the most
> popular men in Saskatchewan. . . . Bankers invite me to dine
> with them. . . . And the evil rich people who looked at me with
> pity last year are now disconcerted. They open their eyes in
> astonishment, they are alarmed, they are angry.[11]

From the beginning, the prime minister was aware of Riel's interest in money and his intention to press his own claims. Macdonald wrote to the governor general in August that Riel "spoke of some claims he had against the government. I presume these refer to his land claims which he forfeited on conviction [sic] and banishment. I think we shall deal liberally with him and make him a good subject again."[12] Accepting Lord Lansdowne's advice to "obtain touch" of Riel,[13] Macdonald instructed Dewdney to sound him out. The first occasion which presented itself was the visit of Bishop Grandin to St. Laurent in the first week of September 1884. He was to be accompanied by A.-E. Forget, who was to see if Riel could be satisfied.

What transpired on this visit is not entirely clear. Louis Schmidt, whose information came from Father André, reported that Bishop Grandin suggested to Riel that he take a place on the Territorial Council, and Riel replied that he would be dishonored if he accepted such a position. He wanted a portfolio in the federal ministry, nothing more or less. Yet Riel's advisers, Maxime Lépine and Charles Nolin, were pressuring him to accept the offer of a seat on the Council, for they thought he could not get more. Lépine also intended to get on the Council, through election, while Nolin wanted to be appointed an Indian agent. Schmidt's reaction was one of disgust: "See our fine national movement leading to the garbage dump! Jobs for the agitators and nothing else. What a farce!"[14]

The account of Nolin and Lépine, while not identical, corroborates Schmidt's version in important respects. Riel told them to see Forget before he did, since he expected an offer might be made. Forget mentioned to Octave Régnier, the local school teacher, that Riel might like Pascal Breland's place on the Territorial Council, at a salary of $1,000 a year. While Régnier passed this on to Nolin and Lépine, Riel went by himself to see Forget, Grandin, and André. They tried to make him accept a place on the Council, but he refused. When Nolin and Lépine reproached him for dealing behind their backs, he said: "Pensez-vous que je voudrais tacher mon nom en allant dans une place de même?" [Do you think I'd ruin my reputation by going to a place like that?] Nolin and Lépine added that Riel often said he would not be surprised to be offered a position in the cabinet or to be made lieutenant-governor.[15]

A slightly different version emerges from accounts on the government side. Forget wrote to Dewdney: "Mr. Riel intends putting in his own personal claims to land in the Province of Manitoba; and also has a claim of indemnity."[16] Dewdney, personally briefed by Forget and Grandin, wrote about the matter to the prime minister. He reported that Riel had been "much quieter" when he spoke privately to Forget. He said the Métis would be satisfied if the recommendations of the North-West Council for a distribution of scrip were followed; if

Nolin were appointed Indian agent; and if he and Lépine became members of the Council. Riel had added: "I do not say that I would give up the United States, I have not made up my mind, and if I did not, then I should want a sum of money."[17]

We shall never know exactly what was said, but certain things are evident: Riel was pursuing his personal objectives at the same time as he forwarded the claims of the *Métis*. His close advisers were well aware of this and indeed had personal interests of their own. The government was also conscious of these individual claims and was willing to consider some sort of arrangement — certainly not a formal admission of fault in its past treatment of Riel, but perhaps an appointment to the Territorial Council. Riel, however, seems to have set his sights higher.

No information is available about Riel's personal claims during October and November, but they reappeared in December, when he apparently began to worry again about his poverty. He had foreclosed his option of returning to Montana to resume teaching, and now the long-awaited petition to Ottawa was almost finished. What would he do next? His concern was evident in this diary entry, which recorded a divine revelation:

> Do not waste anything.
> Riel! Try to provide for your own support. For I do not have the means to see to your livelihood.
> Riel! Do not be afraid. Do not compromise the cause of good. And God will lead you as if by the hand.
> You will lack nothing; if necessary, angels will come to feed you while you sleep. . . .[18]

Throughout December and January Riel's attempts to have his personal claims satisfied took priority over any work on behalf of the *Métis*. The story can be pieced together from accounts left by Charles Nolin, Father André, Louis Schimdt, and D. H. Macdowall, member of the Territorial Council for the District of Lorne.[19] The major sources are really Nolin and André; for Schmidt knew only what he had heard from André, and Macdowall, though he talked to Riel himself, was brought in by André. How reliable are these sources? Nolin's various accounts are open to question, because they were given after the Rebellion, when he had long since broken with Riel and become a star witness for the prosecution. Initially held under strong suspicion when he fled to Prince Albert, Nolin had a powerful incentive to exculpate himself by making Riel look venal. However, his story has the virtue of consistency; it did not change over the three times he told it. Furthermore, his account is not in any important way incompatible with André's, and André cannot be considered a biased witness. Believing Riel insane and also believing that the government had mismanaged the *Métis* problems, he wished to save Riel from the gallows. He was called to testify by the defense at Riel's trial, and the story of Riel's personal claims was only dragged out of him by the Crown attorneys. Furthermore, André's accounts after the Rebellion are quite consistent with the letters he wrote in December and January. Hence we must conclude that the following story, while perhaps open to challenge in some details, rests on strong evidence.

According to Nolin and Lépine, Riel began to speak about money in early December:

> Towards December 7 or 8, Riel showed a desire to have money. He needed five or six thousand dollars. Nolin and Maxime polled those who expected scrip to see if that much could be found. [Riel] told us the government owed him money. Then Nolin said: "There. Now we can have peace. I accept his arguments that the government owes him money."[20]

Nolin told more or less the same story when he testified at Riel's trial, except that he mentioned an initial figure of $10,000 or $15,000 as what Riel wanted. He also added Riel's opinion "that the Canadian Government owed him about $100,000."[21]

On 12 December Riel called on Father André, when the priest was at St. Laurent, and asked for a private interview. He said that he feared an armed rising, that he could no longer control the *Métis*, and that the Indians would support them if they rebelled. He wanted to go back to the United States under the "specious pretext" of negotiating with Canada. He also said he might move to Quebec. When he asked André to get him some money, the priest refused to act alone, but said he would bring in D. H. Macdowall.[22]

This account, written by André several months after the fact, is corroborated by what Louis Schmidt wrote the very day of 12 December, after speaking to André, who had just returned from St. Laurent to Prince Albert:

> Father André has just arrived from St. Laurent, and he has spoken with this unfortunate man [Riel], who, after having defended impractical theories and the most heterodox opinions for a long time, finally gave in and admitted to Father André that he was in an impasse, and that he wanted to get out of it at any price. He asked him to get in touch with Mr. McDowall, that the latter might try to get from the government a certain sum of money to permit him to leave the country, while making the

public believe he was going as a delegate to the Federal government.[23]

It was not new for Riel to speak of his claims; the novelty was in the suggestion that he might separate his own interests from those of the Métis and even create a false impression in order to obtain money. There is no evidence that André forced these ideas on Riel.

André, who very much wanted to get Riel out of the country, quickly contacted Macdowall. The two went to St. Laurent 22 December and saw Riel the next day. He came accompanied by Nolin and Lépine, but those two were not actually present when he spoke with André and Macdowall, a meeting which lasted three or four hours. Both André and Macdowall have left detailed accounts of the conversation, which must be quoted at some length.

According to André, Riel rehearsed his grievances for Macdowall's benefit. He confessed his fears of being unable to control the Métis, and repeated his promise to leave the North-West and go to Quebec, for which he expected "some compensation, not as a bribe but as an indemnity for all the losses he had suffered from being obliged to abandon his country for so long." He wanted $100,000, but not necessarily all at once. "I ask thirty-five thousand dollars paid as soon as I am in Canada, the balance of the sum I will wait for at the convenience of the government." He would take even less than $35,000 as a down payment. He would wait a month or at most forty days for an answer from the government. When Macdowall asked him if this would satisfy the Métis, Riel replied: "Mr. Macdowall, if I am satisfied the Half breeds will be satisfied."[24]

Macdowall's account of the proceedings appeared in a letter he wrote to Governor Dewdney the next day.[25] It agreed exactly with André's version except that Macdowall also inserted his own cynical interpretation of Riel's motives:

> He then proceeded to state that if the Govt. would consider his personal claims against them and pay him a certain amount in settlement of these claims he would arrange to make his illiterate and unreasoning followers well satisfied with almost any settlement of their claims for land grants that the Govt. might be willing to make, and also that he would leave the N.W. never to return. He would like to see Sir John Macdonald himself, and go to Ottawa or elsewhere for this purpose: but to do this it was necessary he should have some money to pay his expenses, as he was poor and had not a cent.

After describing offers made to him by the government in the 1870s, Riel continued, according to Macdowall:

His claims amount to the modest sum of $100,000.00, but he will take $35,000.00 as originally offered [by Father Proulx in 1873], and I believe myself that $3,000.00 to $5,000.00 would cart the whole Riel family across the boundary. Riel made it most distinctly understood that "self" was his main object, and he was willing to make the claim of his followers totally subservient to his own interests. . . . Riel's last statement was that he would not believe in any promise that might be made to him but that if money were sent for him he would carry out his part. He said, "My name is Riel and I want material," which I suppose was a pun. He wished the money principally as a provision for his wife and family in case of his death.

Macdowall did not really seem to think that Riel would cause much trouble, at least until elections for the Territorial Council next spring. Yet there was some cause for worry because Riel "is crafty and from the way he is willing to sacrifice his followers' interests, double-dealing." However, Macdowall did not make a clear recommendation to Governor Dewdney that Riel's demands should be met.

Father André was not so reticent. He wrote to Dewdney shortly afterwards in support of Riel's proposal.

Riel is anxious to leave and we must provide him with the means of leaving; he has certainly certain claims against the Government and those claims must be settled in some way. . . .
Now he seems willing to put all the influence he enjoys on the side of the government if he gets the help he requires. He asks thirty thousand dollars as a first instalment, but obtain for him four or five thousand dollars and I am bold in saying Mr. Macdowall and I will make him agree to any conditions.

André added that if Riel was satisfied, the Métis would vote for Macdowall in the next election "and we will carry everything before us." However, getting Riel out of the country was not all that was required; the Métis would have to get title to their lands and have a few other problems dealt with. But this would not be too hard as most of the grievances were "fanciful."[26]

Riel's meeting with André and Macdowall was not kept secret. It was known the very next day to Inspector Joseph Howe of the NWMP, stationed at Prince Albert. He wrote to his superior officer, Superintendent Crozier, to report what had happened. He was probably informed by Macdowall himself, for he seemed to share Macdowall's low opinion of Riel's motives. He wrote: "[Riel] says that he has such influence with the Half Breeds, that any rights they think they have, or claims upon the Government would be at once dropped by them if he advised them to do so."[27] In factual terms, there is no difference between Howe's letter and the reports of André and Macdowall.

Riel also informed Charles Nolin of his meeting with Macdowall. What he told him coincides with other accounts, except for one significant difference. Riel claimed that he wished to use the money to go to the United States, found a newspaper, raise an army, and invade Canada. He had concealed this, his true intention, from André:

> . . . if he got the money he would go to the United States and start a paper and raise the other nationalities in the States. He said that before the grass is that high in this country you will see foreign armies in this country. He said I will commence by destroying Manitoba, and then I will come and destroy the North-West and take possession of the North-West.[28]

These were Nolin's words at the trial. He said almost exactly the same thing again in 1886, adding that Riel intended to have William Henry Jackson as a collaborator on his newspaper.[29]

The substance of Nolin's report was later confirmed by Riel himself, when he was visited in prison by the medical commission of Drs. Michael Lavell and F.-X. Valade, posing as journalists. Valade recalled:

> Thus upon Dr. Lavell asking why he had proposed giving up the rebellion if the government would pay him the sum of thirty-five thousand dollars, he answered: "Do I enquire of you how you employ your money? Have I not children to educate and provide for?" And on my asking if it were not his intention to return to the states and establish there a great newspaper, "Oh yes," he exclaimed, "This is my divine mission. I must establish a paper for the spread of my views and plans, and with it I must raise an army of twenty or thirty thousand men to carry out my vocation as a Prophet and to reconquer the northwest which I have been chosen to govern."[30]

It is not easy to interpret these statements. Riel's defense counsel, accepting as true Riel's desire to found a newspaper and raise an army, argued that this mad scheme was further proof of his insanity.[31] The prosecuting attorney, on the other hand, emphasized that Riel told different things to different people, as required by the situation. To André and Macdowall, he merely promised to get himself out of the way; but to Nolin he had to appear militant. Crown counsel argued that this deviousness was further proof of Riel's sanity.[32]

Leaving aside the fruitless non-question of whether Riel was "really" insane, it seems likely that his plans were not fixed in December 1884. He obviously wanted to get what he called his indemnity, but he may not have had a definite idea of what he would do with it.

During the month of January 1885, strenuous attempts were made to get money for Riel. Riel himself kept up the pressure; he came twice to Prince Albert to see if progress had been made, and on other occasions he sent his lieutenants to inquire.[33] In the meantime his poverty was relieved slightly by a collection of sixty dollars made by the Métis and presented to him at a banquet at Batoche on 6 January. The speeches at the banquet, which were reported in Le Manitoba, had no hint of rebellion.[34]

Superintendent Crozier came to see Father André on 4 January, and the priest confirmed the intelligence report earlier filed by Inspector Howe.[35] He was so persuasive that three days later Crozier himself wrote to Dewdney, recommending the idea of a personal payment to Riel as well as a prompt settlement of the Métis claims.[36]

Riel came to Prince Albert on 14-15 January with Nolin and Lépine.[37] He saw André and may also have seen Macdowall. At any rate, the latter wrote again to Dewdney on 14 January. He stressed that Riel's presence was bad for immigration and thus for the general prosperity of the country. He urged the government "to at once settle Riel's claims if there be justice in them." If not, the government should openly declare that Riel would get nothing so as to bring the matter to a head. Police reinforcements would be advisable in the latter case. Macdowall was careful never to commit himself to favoring an indemnity for Riel, but he quite sensibly wanted the whole thing settled quickly.[38]

Father André wrote again to Dewdney on 21 January. Less cautious than Macdowall, he asserted that Riel "really has a right" to an indemnity. But the main argument was pragmatic.

> Riel is very anxious to know to know if any decision has arrived, and he has a mind to go down East, if he hears nothing favourable to him. I really think that he is sincere in his desire to remain quiet and to use his influence among the Half breeds for peace if he is satisfied. I know he is much pinched just now and requires greatly help. The man is able to do a great deal of harm "s'il est poussé à la dernière extrémité" ["if he is pushed to the limit,"], as we say in French, so I strongly advise not to look to some paltry thousand dollars when the peace of the country is at stake.[39]

On 27 January an ominous event occurred. Charles Nolin and Maxime Lépine had submitted a tender on a contract to supply poles for a telegraph line between Duck Lake and Edmonton. The money for the project had been advanced by Macdowall. Now, two days before the bids were to be opened, Riel and Gabriel Dumont insisted that Nolin and Lépine withdraw from the competition. In Nolin's words, Riel "asked me to resign him my contract to show the Government that the half-breeds were not satisfied, because the government had not given Riel what he asked for."[40] Nolin allegedly countered by proposing a bargain. He would withdraw his bid if Riel would give up his plan of going to the United States to raise an army, if he would renounce his American citizenship, and if he would run for the House of Commons as soon as ridings would be created in the North-West. According to Nolin, Riel agreed to these conditions, and Dumont and Lépine witnessed the agreement.[41]

Riel gave a slightly different account in his first trial oration. He admitted pressing Nolin to withdraw his bid, but described it as having been done more for the movement as a whole than for his personal claims. He also denied that he had agreed to renounce his American citizenship.[42]

When Nolin went to Prince Albert to give Macdowall back his money, he told him Riel was a dangerous man and advised him to wire the government quickly.[43] Father André, also alarmed by these events, gave the same advice, and Macdowall complied on 3 February.[44] Telegrams also came in from Crozier asking that the claims of Riel and the *Métis* be settled.[45] André himself wrote a third and last time on 6 February. This time he wrote in French in a tone that was a good deal less deferential.

> Le gouvernement a grand tort de ne pas se prêter à ces arrangements, qui serait si utile pour tout le monde. . . . Monsieur le Gouverneur, vous pouvez désormais rester tranquille. C'est la dernière lettre que j'écris à votre honneur à ce sujet. J'ai déjà écrit deux lettres, mais je présume que vous ne les avez pas reçues, puis qu'aucun mot de votre part ne m'en a accusé reception; j'espère que cette troisième lettre et la dernière aura meilleure chance, et qu'elle arrivera à sa destination."
> [The government is making a big mistake in not accepting these arrangements, which would be so useful for everyone. . . . You will not be disturbed again, Governor. This is the last letter I will write to Your Honor on this subject. I have already written two letters, but I assume you have not received them, because you have not acknowledged them in any way. I hope this third and last letter will have better luck and will reach its destination.][46]

Dewdney, though he had not replied to André, had not been ignoring his letters. He had forwarded them, together with those of Macdowall and Crozier, to the prime minister for decision. He did not express an opinion on the merits of the scheme, but his very reserve was bound to be interpreted as lack of enthusiasm.

Macdonald gave his answer in a letter of 20 February, in which he ruled the proposal out of court:

> We have no money to give Riel and would be obliged to ask for a Parliamentary vote.
> How would it look to be obliged to confess we could not govern the country and were obliged to bribe a man to go away? This would never do. He has a right to remain in Canada and if he conspires we must punish him. That's all.[47]

This answer never reached Riel; in any case it was anti-climactic, for he had already inferred that he would get nothing. On 23 December he had told Macdowall he would wait no more than forty days for a reply from the government, which amounted to a deadline of 1 February. On 4 February, the minister of the interior sent Dewdney the telegram (see Chapter 3) announcing that the government had appointed a commission to enumerate the half-breeds who had not participated in the Manitoba land grant. Riel then entered into the dangerous game of confrontation.

Having embarked on this radical course, he still did not abandon the idea of settling his claims. On 29 April 1885, as General Middleton was camped at Fish Creek and preparing to march on Batoche, Riel was praying God to make Canada negotiate with him. He wanted a treaty for the *Métis* and Indians as well as a settlement for himself. "Make Canada consent to pay me the indemnity which is my due, not a small indemnity but an indemnity which will be just and equitable before God and men!"[48] At his trial, too, Riel asserted his claim for money; and as we have seen, he still proposed it to Drs. Lavell and Valade a week before he was hanged.

Riel broke no law in asking the government for money. Did he act immorally, offering to betray the interests of his followers, in effect selling himself for a bribe? Certainly Macdowall and Macdonald saw it that way, as did Louis Schmidt. On the other hand, the various *Métis* who knew of Riel's actions — including Maxime Lépine, Gabriel Dumont, and even Charles Nolin — did not see it as a sell-out. They must have thought Riel's attempt to gain compensation was compatible with rectification of their own grievances. Lépine and Dumont were loyal to the end; and when Nolin and Riel split, it was over whether or not to take up arms, not over Riel's attempts to get money for himself. But whatever one's moral judgment on the episode, its historical importance cannot be ignored. Riel's desire for money was an integral part of the sequence of causes leading to the Rebellion. It would be historically wrong to interpret his role in the insurrection as arising solely, or even chiefly, from disinterested idealism.

CHAPTER SIX

Riel's Trial

After the end of fighting at Batoche, Louis Riel surrendered on 15 May 1885 and was quickly transported to Regina where he was held in the common jail by the North-West Mounted Police. The government now faced the sensitive problem of what to do with him. A trial for treason was anticipated, but the location raised serious difficulties. Riel's actions had been committed in the North-West Territories, so presumably his trial should take place in that jurisdiction. However, the court system established by the North-West Territories Act was less developed than that available in any of the provinces at that time. The Act did not provide for an indictment to be drawn up by a grand jury, even in a capital case of this sort. The trial jury would be only six rather than the usual twelve. And the presiding officer would not be a tenured judge but a stipendiary magistrate serving at the pleasure of the Crown. Trials for political offenses are contentious at best; to hold one under these circumstances would inevitably raise doubts about its fairness.

A newly discovered document shows that the government was made well aware of the problem. The minister of justice asked the two eminent lawyers who had been appointed Crown prosecutors, Christopher Robinson and B. B. Osler, for their opinion. Their reply, dated 16 June 1885, was frank about the difficulties. It would be "anomalous and inappropriate" to conduct a treason trial in a magistrate's court on an ordinary information, without an indictment. Yet the Act of 1880 did not authorize a grand jury to be empanelled. There were imperial statutes, now more than half a century old, which had authorized trial in Upper or Lower Canada for offenses committed in Rupert's Land, "but a resort to these statutes in view of subsequent legislation would not in our judgment be advisable or safe" (a contention later verified in the appeals made by Riel's attorneys). Robinson and Osler recommended that the best course would be legislation to create a special commission for conducting the trial or "a short act giving the Government power to try the offenders within any part of the Dominion."

Though legally possible, these solutions were also beset with difficulties. Would a trial conducted under such *ad hoc* arrangements be perceived as fair? It is not surprising that the government fell back on the concluding remarks of Robinson and Osler:

> Should this be found inadvisable [i.e. special legislation] the best course in our opinion would be to try under the Act of 1880, following its provision as closely as possible and giving the accused every protection or privilege provided by any law not clearly inconsistent with it.[1]

This course of action was bound to be controversial. From the beginning, the trial had been praised as an example of impartial British justice and condemned as a judicial farce. A few of the more vigorous denunciations by historians are worth citing. A.-H. de Trémaudan said that the cause of the verdict "n'était pas la révolte même du Nord-Ouest mais ce fait . . . l'exécution d'un sujet des loges orangistes, Thomas Scott." [was not the revolt of the North-West but the execution of a member of the Orange order, Thomas Scott.][2] Joseph Kinsey Howard wrote: "There can be little question that the circumstances of Louis Riel's trial were immoral. Whether the trial itself was also illegal has been debated ever since it was held."[3] More recently, L. H. Thomas has argued:

> Many laymen who see Riel as a mentally disturbed being call the execution of 1885 a judicial murder. This is perhaps an over-dramatic description of what was essentially a political trial. The government, exploiting the venerable sanctions of an outmoded legality, arranged a trial which satisfied most of the technical requirements of the legal process, but which in reality was designed to assuage the paranoiac fears and passions of Ontario voters.[4]

The question is of more than academic interest. If these views are even approximately correct, Canada would have much to be ashamed of; and presumably the government should grant Riel a posthumous pardon, as requested by the Association of Métis and Non-Status Indians of Saskatchewan. They state flatly that "Riel did not receive a fair trial because of bias and prejudice toward him from many quarters."[5]

A serious study of the fairness of Riel's trial has to meet two standards. First, it has to place the trial within the context of law and judicial practice existing in 1885. It is too easy to introduce anachronistic judgments based on contemporary experience. How often have we not read statements such as: "That Riel was insane enough to satisfy modern legal and medical criteria hardly now seems in question"?[6] Such judgments are meaningless; for, if Riel lived when "modern legal and medical criteria" applied, he would not be the same person. The chance of anachronism is especially great now that treason, in our tolerant (or faint-hearted) era of Western civilization, is almost never prosecuted as such, except perhaps in wartime. Second, such a study must evaluate the rules of conduct followed by participants in the trial, but not the outcome of the trial. A trial is an open process, an elaborate game. Like all such processes, it can be described as fair or unfair to the extent to which participants follow or fail to follow acknowledged rules of procedure. Strictly speaking, there is no such thing as a fair or unfair outcome; there is only a fair (impartial) or unfair (biased) process.[7] The hypothetical question to be answered is whether Riel was tried in the same way as would any other man who had committed similar actions in the same jurisdiction. The point is elementary, but it needs to be made; for it is obvious that many people who have written about the trial begin from a conviction that Riel should or should not have been convicted, and judge the trial accordingly.

Some important work on the subject has already been done. Sandra Bingaman purposely ignored Riel's case in order to concentrate on the other seventy-one Rebellion trials; but many of her findings are relevant to Riel's trial, since it was part and parcel of the whole set of prosecutions. After reviewing such factors as the judges' behavior in the trials, opportunities afforded to defense counsel, and overall adherence to rules of procedure, she concluded that in general, "although errors and inconsistencies were present, there was a serious attempt on the part of all involved to serve the cause of justice."[8] She showed that Judge Hugh Richardson, in particular, made a number of erratic rulings, which, however, favored the defense as often as the prosecution. Beyond that, the "errors and inconsistencies" uncovered in her research chiefly pertained to the trials of the Indian defendants, many of whom were tried without proper interpreters and defense counsel. The Métis and white defendants, including Riel, were much more carefully handled. In another valuable study, D. H. Brown showed clearly that it was not improper to charge Riel with high treason under 25 Edward III, c.2 (the Statute of Treasons, 1352), and

that Riel's American citizenship made no significant difference.[9]
Other recent articles cannot be accepted without reservation. R. E.
Turner[10] and L. H. Thomas[11] have mistakenly introduced the question
of a pre-trial hearing of fitness to stand trial; such a hearing was
impossible under the circumstances. Furthermore, L. H. Thomas and
Desmond Morton[12] have created false impressions about the venue,
suggesting that Riel could (and perhaps should) have been sent to
Winnipeg for trial. The following chronology will help the reader
follow the analysis of issues raised by Riel's trial:

15 May	Riel surrenders.
23 May	Riel arrives in Regina.
12 June	Riel accepts F. X. Lemieux and Charles Fitzpatrick as defense counsel.
6 July	Riel is charged with treason on an information laid by A. D. Stewart.
16 July	Counsel see Riel for the first time.
20 July	Trial begins.
21 July	Judge Richardson grants one week delay for defense to prepare its case.
28 July	Trial resumes.
1 August	Riel is convicted of treason and sentenced to hang on 18 September.
9 September	Manitoba Court of Queen's Bench denies Riel's appeal.
22 October	Judicial Committee of the Privy Council denies Riel's appeal.
9 November	Medical commission telegraphs reports to prime minister about Riel's sanity.
16 November	Riel is hanged at Regina.

COMPARISON WITH OTHER TREASON TRIALS

Since Riel was the only prisoner tried for high treason in the
seventy-two Rebellion trials, it is useful to view his case within the
broader context of nineteenth-century treason trials. How does the
development of the trial itself and particularly its duration compare
with other trials? Was the sentence unusually harsh? Was it executed
unusually quickly?

It has been observed that the trial of Louis Riel is the most famous
trial in Canadian history.[13] As a trial for high treason, however, it was
not unique. Of the two hundred and forty-six British and Canadian
trials for high treason examined in a recent study by Flanagan and

Watson,[14] one hundred and fifty-five were Canadian, most arising from the Ancaster Assize of 1814 and the Upper and Lower Canadian Rebellion trials of 1838. This is a significant body of litigation, which provides some standards with which to compare features of Riel's.[15]

Was the trial of Louis Riel unduly fast by contemporary standards? The question is particularly important because in popular Canadian mythology, "Riel was hurried to the gallows by bigoted Orangemen."[16] The average length of Canadian treason trials prior to Riel's about which information can be secured was just over twenty days from arraignment to sentencing. The average length of treason trials in Canada and Great Britain was just over twenty-one days.

One might conclude that the typical Canadian or British trial was somewhat longer and perhaps fairer when compared to the twelve days of Riel's trial. However, procedural differences influenced the varying lengths of trials. Riel's trial proceedings were necessarily abbreviated since there was no provision in the North-West Territories for a grand jury. Also, most nineteenth-century treason trials brought a group of, say, twenty to thirty accused traitors to the bar for arraignment together, while their trials were held over the course of successive days. Statistically, the misleading impression arises that the last in a series of accused traitors benefited from a "trial" of several weeks, when the hearing itself may have been extremely brief. Interestingly, the duration of Riel's hearing compares favorably with other trials. The average length of hearing for all the trials studied by Flanagan and Watson was slightly less than one and one-half days, or three and one-half days less than Riel received. Indeed, no trial other than Riel's could be found in which the hearing exceeded three days.

The Statute of Treasons under which Riel was tried provided for only one penalty: death. Strictly speaking, it would be illogical to compare his sentence to that of others who were tried under different statutes allowing various penalties. However, after the jury convicted Riel and the judge passed the mandatory death sentence, it was always open to the governor general, with or even without the advice of the cabinet, to commute the sentence to a lesser penalty. Thus in a general way it makes sense to compare Riel's ultimate fate to that of others convicted of treason.

Though the full measure of the death sentence was carried out in the first Canadian case of high treason,[17] the precedent was not consistently followed in subsequent trials. Of the seventeen found guilty by the Ancaster Assize of 1814, ten were hanged. Twenty-four years later, in the wake of the Upper Canadian rebellion, all twenty-eight tried for high treason at the Hamilton Special Assize were pardoned, conditionally or otherwise.[18] Twelve of the one hundred and eight brought forward in the Lower Canadian trials were executed, the remainder being freed under bond, acquitted, or deported to Australia.[19] In the aggregate, since less than fifteen percent of all those found guilty of high treason in nineteenth-century Canada were executed, one can conclude that Canadian courts were inclined to display leniency. However, a different picture emerges from a survey of sentences in British treason trials. Almost one-half of those tried for high treason were put to death, and the law reports are replete with cases in which most or all of the trials arising from individual rebellions or insurrections resulted in execution.[20] The wisdom of Riel's death sentence may be debatable, but the sentence itself was not anomalous by the standards of contemporary British justice.

Riel's treatment was unique with respect to the time taken to carry out the sentence. The one hundred and seven days from 1 August through 16 November, 1885, to allow appeals to be taken to the Manitoba Court of Queen's Bench and the Judicial Committee of the Privy Council, as well as an inquiry by a medical commission, stand in sharp contrast to the average time of twenty-five days allowed in other treason cases.[21] Moreover, in spite of earlier attempts in England to extend the interval between the pronouncement and accomplishment of sentence, instances of execution on the day following sentencing are commonplace.[22] It is difficult then to claim that Riel was hurried to the gallows.

TREASON VS. TREASON-FELONY

Legally, Riel could have been charged with either treason or treason-felony. D. H. Brown proved that the charge of treason was legal, but he did not discuss whether treason-felony might have been a more appropriate designation for Riel's actions. Thomas has claimed that the fundamental difference hinged upon whether intended or real acts of war were involved.[23] The actual wording of the statutes, however, reveals very little practical difference in the charges. The Statute of Treasons (1352) states that the accused "did . . . traitorously attempt and endeavour by force and arms to subvert and destroy . . . the . . . government of this realm."[24] The 1868 Canadian treason-felony statute states that one "compasses . . . to levy war against Her Majesty . . . such compassings . . . or intentions . . . shall express . . . by any overt act or deed . . . ."[25] Implicit in this and underscored later in the same statute is that indictments for treason-felony were to be valid though the facts might amount to treason.[26]

In view of the large measure of discretion left to prosecutors,[27] it seems that the standard for judging the appropriateness of Riel's indictment must come from a comparison with other cases. Unfortunately, comparisons with Canadian treason trials are impossible since the statute by which treason-felony was introduced into Canadian law did not exist before 1868 and was not extended to the North-West Territories until 1873.[28] In the United Kingdom, however, treason-felony as an alternative to the charge of high treason dates from 1848.[29] Significantly, in the twenty-three trials for treason-felony examined by Flanagan and Watson, none of the indictments involved acts of war or insurrection. Seven resulted from the possession of arms or explosives for the purpose of insurrection, while the remaining sixteen indictments involved seditious publications. Alleged responsibility for actual insurrection or acts of war related mainly to Fenian activity resulted in indictments for high treason.[30] Thus an indictment for treason-felony for Riel's participation in the armed rebellion in the North-West would have been unusually lenient in view of precedent in the United Kingdom. However, the government did exhibit some leniency in charging Riel's *Métis* followers with treason-felony. There seems to have been an element of plea-bargaining here, as several *Métis* agreed to plead guilty to treason-felony if they would not be charged with high treason.[31] It is not clear whether the prosecution would actually have made the stronger charge, and whether convictions upon it could have been obtained.

VENUE

Riel's own ideas about venue differed from those of his counsel, who argued that the territorial court did not have jurisdiction over his case and that he should be tried in Ontario. He telegraphed instructions to his counsel: "Pray well federal government to grant my trial before Supreme Court and in Lower Canada."[32] He made the same request in letters to Governor Dewdney. The rationale was that he envisioned a hearing on his entire career, from the first uprising of 1869 through the tangled issues of the amnesty question down to the most recent events of 1885. The people of Quebec would be more acquainted with his career than the inhabitants of other parts of Canada.[33] But there was no legal mechanism by which the Supreme Court of Canada could be the court of original jurisdiction in a case of this sort, much less in the province of Quebec.

A new theory about the venue emerged with the publication of the *Telegrams of the North-West Campaign*, which shows that the government first instructed General Middleton to send Riel to Winnipeg. A few days later the minister of militia telegraphed Middleton to change the destination to Regina.[34] These facts, coupled with interpretation of some correspondence by the minister of justice, have led to the view that the government had an option of trying Riel in either Winnipeg or Regina. The former venue was supposedly rejected because there Riel could have demanded a "mixed" jury of twelve, that is, half English and half French. The impression is given by Morton and especially by Thomas[35] that the Regina venue was a deliberate, if belated, decision by the government to ensure that Riel would be tried before an English-speaking jury.

If this interpretation were valid, it would be curious that no one raised the issue at the time of the trial. In fact it is based on an anachronistic misconstruction of the law. The North-West Territories Act of 1873 had provided that crimes punishable by death and arising in the North-West should be tried in Manitoba, and this provision was retained in the amended Act of 1875.[36] But it was dropped from the Act of 1880,[37] where the powers of stipendiary magistrates in the North-West were expanded. It was never expressly repealed,[38] but it is not unusual for statute law to lapse without explicit repeal. There is no evidence that anyone in 1885 regarded the provision as alive.

Close reading of the letters to Macdonald from Alexander Campbell,[39] minister of justice, suggests that the initial decision to send Riel to Winnipeg was recommended by Minister of Militia Adolphe Caron, on military grounds. He was afraid that Riel and the other Métis prisoners would be exposed to rescue attempts at Regina. To be sure, Campbell, who consistently pressed for a Regina venue, tried to sway the prime minister by pointing out the existence of Manitoba's system of "mixed" juries. But he also raised the question of whether a Manitoba trial was even legally possible. On 21 May he wrote that the lieutenant-governor of Manitoba had requested advice about the authority under which to receive Riel. "I shall be obliged to reply that there is no authority,"[40] Campbell concluded.

The correspondence does not reveal a vengeful determination to "fix" Riel's trial by depriving him of French jurors. It shows instead a confused cabinet: a single-minded minister of militia who knows nothing of the judicial issues and will not listen to the minister of justice; a minister of justice who is not certain of the law and seems to have no reliable advisers in Ottawa (he has to appeal to the chief justice of Manitoba for information); and a prime minister who does not know that Regina is on the rail line, who forgets that he has received and answered memos, and who has to be badgered into taking action. It was lucky that a legally correct decision emerged at the end.

Incidentally, it appears that Riel could have been tried anywhere within the North-West Territories, since the Act of 1880 was silent about venue. The tradition of British justice is to hold trials close to where the alleged crimes were committed, which might have suggested Battleford or Prince Albert as a venue. Regina was chosen by the government for reasons of convenience and security, but the choice does not seem legally unfair. Regina was arguably a more neutral venue than Battleford or Prince Albert, which had been under siege for several months.

FITNESS TO STAND TRIAL

R. E. Turner has pointed out that if Riel were to be tried today, he would almost certainly receive a pre-trial hearing to consider his fitness to stand trial.[41] Such a hearing would investigate his sanity at the present moment, in contrast to a plea of innocent by reason of insanity, which considers the defendant's mental condition at the time the crime was allegedly committed. Turner further suggested that Riel could have had such a pre-trial hearing. He cited the Act relating to Procedure in Criminal Cases in Canada of 1869, c.29, s.102:

> If any person indicted for any offense be insane, and upon arraignment be so found by a jury empanelled for that purpose, so that such person cannot be tried upon such indictment, or if, upon the trial of any person so indicted, such person appears to the jury charged with the indictment to be insane, the Court, before whom such person is brought to be arraigned, may direct such finding to be recorded, and thereupon may order such person to be kept in strict custody until the pleasure of the Lieutenant-Governor be known.[42]

This point was subsequently picked up by Thomas, who wrote: "One can only speculate why Riel's lawyers did not at the beginning of the proceedings raise the question of his fitness to stand trial, since an insane person cannot be tried."[43] However, there is no mystery here. Rules of criminal procedure in Canada applied in the North-West Territories only if they had been extended by statute to that jurisdiction. This provision had not been extended by 1885,[44] making a pre-trial fitness hearing legally dubious, if not impossible. This would explain why the issue was not raised at Riel's trial, nor indeed until eighty years later, when the passage of time had encouraged anachronistic interpretation.

Incidentally, this point makes possible a better understanding of the trial of William Henry Jackson. Everyone (except Jackson himself) was convinced that he was insane at the time of the trial: his family, the doctors who examined him, his defense counsel, prosecuting attorneys, and officials of the Department of Justice. Yet under the prevailing rules of procedure, he had to be tried. His attorneys entered a plea of not guilty by reason of insanity, which in theory required them to establish Jackson's incompetence during the Rebellion. But the only witnesses called by the defense were Drs. Jukes and Cotton, who both testified that Jackson "would not now, in his present condition, be accountable for any actions he might perform." The Crown attorneys could have destroyed this defense, had they wished; but they were happy to cooperate in getting Jackson out of the way, and he was despatched to Lower Fort Garry on a lieutenant-governor's warrant.[45]

In effect, Jackson received a hearing on his fitness to stand trial; but it was conducted under the form of a trial, and the jury found a verdict of "not guilty on the ground of insanity." This peculiar trial has always drawn unfavorable comment because of its obviously illogical conduct. The general opinion that Jackson got off rather easily is highly questionable. If Jackson had received a trial on the facts of the case, his participation in the Rebellion would have been shown to be slight at best. He took no hostages nor participated in any battles. Contrary to what is often said, he was not the secretary of the Exovedate. He wrote a few letters for Riel before the battle of Duck Lake, some of which were probably seditious. Once the fighting started, Riel and the other *Métis* lost confidence in him, and he became merely one of the hostages. In a trial where all the facts were brought out, he might have been convicted of treason-felony; but in view of Judge Richardson's relative leniency in sentencing, he would probably have drawn a short term in Stony Mountain penitentiary. As it was, he was put in a lunatic asylum for an indefinite term — a potentially harsher fate. The situation resembles modern abuses of pre-trial hearing which have been criticized by civil libertarians.

COMPOSITION OF THE JURY

The North-West Territories Act (1880) established the following procedure for jury selection.

> Persons required as jurors for a trial shall be summoned by a Stipendiary Magistrate from among such male persons as he may think suitable in that behalf; and the jury required on such trial shall be called from among the persons so summoned as such jurors, and sworn by the Stipendiary Magistrate who presides at the trial.[46]

Further sections of the Act set forth rules regarding challenges for cause as well as peremptory challenges (six for the accused, four for the Crown).

Judge Richardson caused a jury panel of thirty-six men to be summoned for the trial. It is not known exactly how the names were selected,[47] but they showed a considerable geographical dispersion from east to west in their home location (from R1W2 to R28W2). However, they were less dispersed from north to south; all came from the band of townships 16-21 lying roughly along the CPR line. Only two of the names (Limoges, Fregent) seemed French, which is not a surprising result for the area included, since most of the French settlements in the Territories lay farther north. To have more French names on the panel, Richardson would have had to call jurors from much farther away or deliberately to seek out French names from nearby settlements like Qu'Appelle. Both procedures would have been obnoxious to the British tradition of randomly calling jurors from the neighborhood of the trial. When the trial opened, one French member of the panel — Benjamin Limoges — did not appear. The defense then challenged five names and the prosecution one.[48] The resulting jury was composed entirely of men of British stock — almost a foregone conclusion in view of the population from which it had been selected.

Several observations must be made against the common view that this jury was somehow "stacked" against Riel. First, the procedures specified in the North-West Territories Act were followed scrupulously. Second, it is not known whether the panel of thirty-six was similar in ethnic composition to other panels normally called at Regina around this time. I am not aware of any statistical or archival information which would offer a comparative perspective on Riel's jury. Finally, those who criticize the composition of the jury seem to assume that a fair trial is impossible unless the jurors are an ethnic microcosm of some larger population. This principle is highly dubious and has never been enshrined in Canadian law, except for the existence of bilingual juries in Quebec and Manitoba. And it was just such a bilingual jury which in 1874 convicted Ambroise Lépine of the murder of Thomas Scott.

JURISDICTION

At the outset of the trial, Riel's lawyers challenged the jurisdiction of the Territorial magistrate's court, arguing that their client must be tried in Ontario or British Columbia. They supported this contention with two major arguments.

The first had to do with trial by jury. Under the procedures set up by the North-West Territories Act of 1880, there was no grand jury and the trial jury was to be composed of only six men, not the twelve usually employed in British criminal cases. Further, the Act allowed the jury panel to be selected by the magistrate himself and the defense was limited to six challenges, as compared to twenty in Britain. Finally, the magistrate presiding over the trial was not an independent, tenured judge but a stipendiary magistrate serving at the pleasure of the government and thus open to possible political pressure. For all these reasons, said Charles Fitzpatrick, one of Riel's counsel, "It is true that we have trial by jury. But it is the shadow and not the substance."[49] Fitzpatrick argued that trial by jury in criminal cases was a constitutional right of British subjects, well established since Magna Carta. No legislature could take it away or weaken it substantially. Hence the North-West Territories Act was *ultra vires* of the Dominion Parliament in those provisions that set up a modified jury system.

Strictly speaking, this argument implied that no legislature, not even the Imperial Parliament, could violate the British constitution by creating such a jury system as existed in the North-West Territories. However, Riel's counsel did not have to emphasize this challenge to the doctrine of parliamentary supremacy because of their second argument, which focused on the legislative competence of the Dominion Parliament in Territorial affairs. They contended that prior Imperial legislation, which had never been repealed, prevented the Dominion from conducting trials for capital offenses in the North-West Territories.

In 1821 the Imperial Parliament had passed "An Act for regulating the fur trade and establishing a criminal and civil jurisdiction within certain parts of North America."[50] Although the statute provided for courts in Rupert's Land, it did not confer upon these courts jurisdiction in cases involving capital punishment. Defendants in such cases were to be sent for trial to Upper Canada. The legislation had been passed to deal with the unique events of the struggle between the North-West Company and the Hudson's Bay Company, including the battle of Seven Oaks; but it remained on the statute books long afterwards and the relevant sections (like that on trial venue in the 1873 North-West Territories Act) had not been expressly repealed as of 1885. In 1859, an additional statute had confirmed the former while adding to it the possibility of a trial in British Columbia for capital cases.[51] If these two laws were still in force, Riel could be tried, but not in Regina or anywhere else in the North-West Territories.

There was evidently a conflict between Imperial legislation and Dominion legislation. In the view of Riel's counsel, Imperial legislation had to take precedence, not only from general considerations but from the wording of another Imperial statute of 1865, "An Act to remove doubts as to the validity of Colonial Laws."[52] This law clearly stated that colonial legislation which was repugnant to any act of the British Parliament was invalid. Now the Dominion Parliament could legislate for the North-West Territories only in virtue of authority delegated to it first by the Rupert's Land Act of 1868 and second by the British North America Act of 1871 which confirmed the validity of the transfer of Rupert's Land, even though it had taken place under the irregular conditions of the Red River Resistance of 1869-70. Thus the Dominion had no legislative competence which had not been delegated by the Imperial Parliament and which was not bound by the interpretation statute of 1865.

Counsel for the Crown offered rebuttal of both arguments made by the defense. As to the constitutional right of trial by jury, Christopher Robinson said: "Neither the right of grand jury nor the petit jury, nor the right of a jury of any kind, is so much a fundamental principle of the British constitution as the supremacy of Parliament."[53] He cited an earlier Canadian case which showed that the courts would not overturn otherwise sound legislation on grounds of violating natural justice or other such theoretical criteria.[54] The question was accordingly whether or not the Dominion Parliament had the competence to legislate as it had. The answer was yes. The statute of 1821, though never expressly repealed, was no longer in force: "we all know perfectly well that there is a large number of statutes which, though not expressly repealed in words, are in effect repealed, because, by virtue of the subsequent legislation and of their inconsistency with the legislation, they have ceased to be in force and have become unnecessary."[55] Robinson went on to cite the Imperial statutes which had explicitly given the Dominion Parliament legislative jurisdiction over Rupert's Land. In the first North-West Territories Act of 1873, Canada had exercised its jurisdiction to provide that capital cases arising in the North-West should be tried in Manitoba, a provision which remained in effect until 1880, when the Territorial courts were given power to try capital cases. Prior to 1885, no one had challenged the validity of these laws. However, a challenge had recently arisen over a murder case tried in Regina, and on appeal the Court of Queen's Bench of Manitoba had confirmed the competence of the Territorial courts to deal with capital cases.[56] Finally, if the defense were correct, the whole system of justice in Manitoba, as well as the Territories, would be undermined. If the statute of 1821 were still valid, capital cases would not be tried in Manitoba any more than in the North-West. Hence, concluded Robinson, "the matter is in great simplicity."[57] Riel could be tried in Regina.

Without explaining his reasons, Judge Richardson accepted the argument of the Crown counsel and allowed the trial to proceed. After conviction, Riel appealed to the Court of Queen's Bench of Manitoba, as provided by the North-West Territories Act (1880). Jurisdiction was a major issue in the appeal, so that all three judges who wrote opinions had to address the question. They unanimously supported the point of view of the prosecution that parliamentary supremacy was more fundamental than trial by jury of a certain size. The attempt of the defense to turn trial by jury of twelve into an entrenched constitutional right they rejected as perhaps appropriate to the American system but not to the flexibility of the unwritten British constitution. On the narrower grounds of the jurisdiction of the Dominion Parliament, they also agreed with the Crown counsel. The authority of the Parliament of Canada, established in the British North America Acts of 1867 and 1871, the Rupert's Land Act of 1868, and other statutes, was complete within its assigned limits, as complete as even the legislative competence of the British Parliament. In the words of Justice Killam, "the plenary powers of legislation conferred upon the Parliament of Canada included the right to alter or to repeal prior Acts of the Imperial Parliament upon subjects upon which the Canadian Parliament is given power to legislate, so far as the internal government of Canada is concerned."[58] Thus the fact that Britain had created certain judicial arrangements in Rupert's Land and had never repealed those arrangements did not prevent Canada from establishing different judicial institutions, once Rupert's Land had passed into its legislative domain.

The unanimous decision of the Court of Queen's Bench of Manitoba was confirmed when the Judicial Committee of the Privy Council refused to entertain a further appeal from Riel's counsel. There was thus consistent judicial opinion, from the lowest to the highest level, that the court before which Riel was tried had legitimate jurisdiction. I do not claim any special knowledge of the intricate constitutional principles involved in the decision, but from a common sense point of view the result seems proper. If Riel's counsel had been correct, not only would the courts of Manitoba and the North-West have been declared illegitimate, but serious doubt might have been cast upon the validity of Dominion legislation in many other fields where Imperial statutes had not been formally repealed. From this vantage point, this challenge of Riel's counsel to the jurisdiction of the court seems like an ingenious case of special pleading.

INSANITY

Apart from the procedural matter of jurisdiction, the main issue at Riel's trial was the substantive question of his sanity. Since medieval times, conviction for criminal offenses under English law has required *mens rea* in the defendant, that is, a guilty intent. Insanity which would make formation of guilty intent impossible has for centuries been a defense to a criminal charge. Riel's counsel defended him in this way, alleging that their client did not have the mental capacity of *mens rea*. Riel, however, rejected their contention, wishing to argue that his actions had been justified by the various misdeeds of the government. When he got the opportunity to speak, he did his best to demolish the insanity plea made by his lawyers, whom he probably would have dismissed if he had had the money to hire replacements. But his own strategy was legally hopeless because a government's mistakes can never be a sufficient defense against the charge of treason, at least as long as the same government continues to rule. Thus the insanity plea made by his attorneys was the only legal issue of the trial once the matter of jurisdiction had been settled.

Two facts make it easy to misinterpret this aspect of the trial. First, medicine and the criminal law have different views of insanity. What doctors will diagnose as incapacitating mental disease and will treat in various ways is not necessarily what courts will regard as a satisfactory defense to criminal charges. Second, definitions of insanity vary considerably among legal systems and within one legal system over periods of time. The question is not simply, was Riel insane? It is, rather, was he insane in the eyes of the criminal law as this concept was understood at the time and place of his trial?

Although insanity had long been a defense to criminal charges in English law, the working definition of insanity had not been precisely formulated. *Arnold's Case* in 1723 had propounded the stringent criterion that to be acquitted "a man must be totally deprived of his understanding and memory, so as not to know what he is doing, no more than an infant, a brute, or a wild beast." The contrary extreme of leniency appeared in 1800 in *Hadfield's Case*, in which a man who tried to kill George III was acquitted because he was "under the influence of insanity at the time the act was committed."[59] The bulk of precedents favored some version of the cognitive test of ability to tell right from wrong, but the law was not firmly settled as late as 1843, when Daniel McNaghten shot and killed the private secretary of Prime Minister Sir Robert Peel. McNaghten had been trying to assassinate the prime minister, for he believed that the Tories were engaged in a conspiracy to persecute him. McNaghten was not a raving lunatic, he was a man who reasoned, spoke, and behaved normally except for his obsession about the prime minister. How was he to be judged? By a cognitive test, he was probably able to distinguish right from wrong and was accountable for his actions. By a volitional test, it was arguable that his delusion had such an effect on his mind as to deprive him of normal free will and hence of the capacity for *mens rea*.

McNaghten was acquitted through the brilliant efforts of his advocate, Alexander Cockburn. Drawing on the emerging discipline of medical psychology, and particularly on the writings of the American alienist Isaac Ray, Cockburn merged the cognitive and volitional tests in an unprecedented way. Insanity could "lead to a partial or total aberration of the moral senses and affections, which may render the wretched patient incapable of resisting the delusion, and lead him to commit crimes for which morally he cannot be held responsible."[60] The phrase "aberration of the moral senses" is cognitive, while "incapable of resisting the delusion" is volitional.

The press, the government, and the queen were indignant to see McNaghten sent to a lunatic asylum rather than hanged. Their outrage caused the House of Lords to take the novel step of calling together the fifteen judges of the common law courts, to pose to them certain questions about the interpretations of criminal insanity. The judges' answers to these questions are the famous McNaghten Rules. For our purposes, the important part of the McNaghten Rules is the following passage:

> to establish a defense on the ground of insanity it must be clearly proved that, at the time of committing the act, the accused was labouring under such a defect of reason, from disease of the mind, as not to know the nature and quality of the act he was doing, or, if he did know it, that he did not know he was doing what was wrong.[61]

These words were not entirely clear. For one thing, they begged the question of whether "wrong" meant legally wrong or morally wrong. A person like McNaghten might recognize that it was illegal to kill the prime minister but might still consider it morally justified. But in spite of such ambiguities, the McNaghten Rules clearly rehabilitated the cognitive approach to insanity.

The legal status of the Rules was anomalous. They were not a precedent arising from a concrete case but an abstract formulation of the law propounded under a certain amount of political pressure. Nonetheless, they were applied during the rest of the century by British judges, in the colonies as well as in the mother country. With repeated usage, they quickly became settled law in spite of their unusual origin. There was, however, continuing opposition to them. The psychiatric profession generally did not accept the cognitive test, which clashed with medical notions of the diseased mind. As a recent book has shown, the dispute involved a clash over professional jurisdictions.[62] The McNaghten Rules, in practice, furnished a strict criterion which relatively few defendants could meet, thus reducing the number of acquittals. This tended to anger alienists, virtually all of whom were asylum directors and whose professional raison d'être would be proportionally enhanced the more criminals could be redefined as lunatics. Whatever the motives of judges, lawyers, and alienists, cases tried under the McNaghten Rules frequently produced scenes of alienists testifying as expert witnesses for the defense, attacking the McNaghten Rules and trying to persuade the jury to acquit the defendant by reason of insanity defined according to some version of the volitional test.

Seen against this background, Riel's case becomes easy to understand. The McNaghten Rules were taken by the presiding judges, both at the trial and the appellate levels, to constitute the law. In his charge to the jury, Judge Richardson quoted the exact words from the McNaghten Rules cited above and concluded: "That I propound to you as the law."[63] Within this framework, the jury had little choice but to convict. Riel was not a gibbering madman who did not know what he was doing. He spoke eloquently to the jury on complex subjects of government and politics. If he seemed obsessed with his divine "mission," the same could have been said of Joseph Smith, William Miller, or other religious innovators of the nineteenth century. Verdun-Jones is surely correct when he writes: "In the light of contemporary interpretations of the insanity test established by the McNaghten Rules there is therefore probably very little doubt that the jury's verdict was eminently predictable."[64]

Riel's lawyers properly did their best to secure an acquittal. They brought in a well-known alienist, Dr. Daniel Clark of Toronto, to examine their client. Not surprisingly, Dr. Clark found Riel insane and not accountable for his actions. However, careful reading of his testimony shows he was operating outside the boundaries of the McNaghten Rules:

Q.   Do you consider, doctor, that a person suffering from such unsoundness of mind as you say this man is suffering from, is incapable of taking the nature of the acts which they do?

A.   Why, the insane understand, many of them, the nature of the acts which they do, except in dementia cases and melancholia and cases of mania even; they often know what they do and can tell all about it afterwards; it is all nonsense to talk about a man not knowing what he is doing, simply because he is insane.

Q.   Do you think that that man was, in the circumstances detailed by the different witnesses, in a position to be able to say or be able to judge of what he was doing as either wrong or contrary to law?

A.   Well, that is one of the legal metaphysical distinctions in regard to right and wrong, and it is a dangerous one, simply because it covers only partly the truth. I could convince any

lawyers if they will come to Toronto Asylum, in half an
hour, that dozens in that institution know right and wrong
both in the abstract and concrete, and yet are undoubtedly
insane; the distinction of right and wrong covers part of the
truth; it covers the larger part of the truth, but the large
minority of the insane do know right from wrong. It is one
of those metaphysical subtleties that practical men in
asylums know to be false.[65]

Under cross-examination, Dr. Clark stated even more plainly, "I think
that he [Riel] knows what right is from wrong, subject to his delusions;
but, mind you, I want to add to that, that many of the insane know
right from wrong."[66] Dr. Clark's testimony could not be convincing to
a jury instructed to deliberate under the McNaghten Rules.

In his final speech for the defense, Charles Fitzpatrick tried to show
a pattern of irrationality in his client's actions. Riel had consistently
acted in a quixotic way because of his disease of "megalomania."[67]
With a pitiful rabble at his back, he had declared war against Canada.
He had surrendered to General Middleton when he could easily have
escaped. He had admittedly tried to get money from the government
before the Rebellion, but that seemingly rational act had been for the
crazy purpose of founding an American newspaper to promote an
invasion of Canada. This argument persuaded neither the jury nor the
appellate judges. The latter were particularly impressed by the
evidence about Riel's attempts to get money from the government.
Chief Justice Wallbridge pointed out that "he was willing and quite
capable of parting with this supposed delusion, if he got the
$35,000."[68] Justice Taylor admitted that Riel had bizarre religious
views, but insisted that "heresy is not insanity."[69] He added that Riel
did not intentionally launch himself on the mad scheme of conducting
warfare against Canada. His plan had been to take hostages and
compel negotiations. "The fighting which actually took place was not
the means by which he had hoped to secure his ends."[70] So his
conduct was not as irrational as Fitzpatrick had suggested.

The modern reader may feel that this was an unjust verdict based
on a faulty conception of insanity. In Canada the law has subsequently
been modified to take a less strictly cognitive view of criminal
responsibility. The Criminal Code of 1892 contained an amended
version of the McNaghten Rules:

No person shall be convicted of an offense by reason of an act
done or omitted by him when labouring under natural
imbecility, or disease of the mind, to such an extent as to render
him incapable of appreciating the nature and quality of the act

or omission, and of knowing that such act or omission was wrong.[71]

The McNaghten requirement to "know the nature and quality of the act" was here replaced by the more permissive phrase of "appreciating the nature and quality of the act." This means that, although a defendant might "know" in some abstract sense that he was doing wrong, he might still be acquitted if his mental condition made it impossible for him to "appreciate" the repercussion of his actions as a normal person might. Under this definition of criminal responsibility, it might be more likely, although hardly certain, that Riel would be acquitted. But under the law which prevailed at the time of the trial, it seems that there was little doubt about the jury's decision.

CONCLUSION

Riel's trial stands up well as an example of the judicial process and was "fair" in the only meaningful sense of that term: namely that the trial was impartially conducted under the prevailing rules of criminal procedure. But the fact that the trial had to be held under the restricted procedures of the North-West Territories Act has prevented, and will probably continue to prevent it, from being universally acknowledged as fair. One can only speculate whether the problem of acceptance would have been so great if the government had accepted the original advice of the Crown counsel to create a special tribunal through legislation.

CHAPTER SEVEN

THE MEDICAL COMMISSION

Up to this point, the record of the government has stood up better to scrutiny than one would have expected from the tone of much that has been written about the Rebellion. The government should be most gravely criticized not so much for the way it dealt with the *Métis* as for the way it dealt with public opinion once the *Métis* had commenced their rising. The prime minister made a number of statements to the House of Commons which were either less or more than the full truth. For example, when he was asked on 23 March 1885 to comment about a *Métis* Bill of Rights reportedly submitted to the government, he replied: "The Bill of Rights had never been officially, or indeed in any way, promulgated so far as we know, and transmitted to the Government."[1] The answer was correct to the extent that it applied to the Bill of Rights which Riel and Jackson were preparing in early winter, 1885; but it was misleading because it ignored the petition sent to the secretary of state, 16 December 1884, as well as all the earlier submissions of the *Métis*. Macdonald's statement left the quite untrue impression that the *Métis* had never tried to bring their grievances to the attention of the government. On 26 March, Macdonald said: "Well, Sir, before Riel came in these settlers had never sent in a Bill of Rights to us, never sent any complaints to the Government."[2] Again, he was playing with the truth. While the settlers had never submitted a document entitled "Bill of Rights," they had certainly sent in many memorials and petitions. On a different but equally deceptive note, the prime minister implied on 6 July that the half-breed rising resulted from a conspiracy of white settlers in the West.[3] A survey of *Hansard* and of the contemporary press would turn up many such untrue, inaccurate, misleading public statements by Macdonald or other

Conservative spokesmen. It must be remembered, however, that these were political statements made as the Conservatives and Liberals waged their contest for mastery of public opinion. Both sides often skirted the truth in what they said. Such distortions do not do the government's reputation any good today, but neither should they obscure the reality of its administrative record in dealing with the grievances of the Métis.

A much more serious episode of dishonesty was the government's handling of the medical commission which was appointed to investigate Riel's sanity before he was hanged. Let us briefly recall the outcome of the trial. Riel's jury found him guilty of high treason but also recommended him "to the mercy of the crown." They suggested clemency not because they believed Riel insane — in which case they should have returned a verdict of not guilty — but because they believed the Rebellion of 1885, while perhaps not justifiable, was understandable in view of the government's dilatory handling of settlers' grievances.[4] Judge Hugh Richardson had no choice under the law but to impose the death sentence, leaving the possibility of pardon to the power of the Crown. But before the cabinet had to confront the question, there were still appeals to be heard. On 9 September the Court of Queen's Bench in Manitoba, and on 22 October the Judicial Committee of the Privy Council refused to set aside Riel's conviction. Now the issue left the judicial realm and entered the political.

For three months pressures had been mounting on the cabinet. From Quebec had come petitions demanding clemency, from Ontario petitions demanding the rigor of the law. Sir John A. Macdonald, faced with the possibility that his Quebec supporters might defect if Riel were executed, used a petition[5] by F.-X. Lemieux, Riel's attorney, for a further examination of his client's mental state as an occasion to placate the French members of the cabinet, particularly J.-A. Chapleau and Hector Langevin. He agreed to commission a medical inquiry into Riel's present sanity. Regardless of his mental condition at the time of his treasonous acts, if he was of unsound mind now, he should not be hanged. There was precedent in British law for such a procedure. It could be carried out in those rare cases where a condemned prisoner was thought to have lost his sanity between sentencing and execution, on the theory that it would be inhumane as well as pointless to execute a lunatic who could not understand the reason for his punishment. More commonly, the procedure was used where the government had reservations about the court's determination that a condemned prisoner was responsible for the crime he had committed.[6] The post-trial inquiry into the prisoner's sanity could furnish the government a plausible reason to exercise the royal prerogative of mercy without attempting to overturn the verdict of the court.

On 23 October, Sir Alexander Campbell, former minister of justice, had written to the prime minister putting forward the name of Dr. Michael Lavell, warden of the Kingston Penitentiary. "Lavell alone is what I would like — a quiet enquiry and report without loss of time — no one to know. To send up three men would be blazoned abroad and result in disagreement and fresh difficulty."[7] Lavell would indeed have been a congenial choice for the prime minister. A devout Methodist and staunch Conservative, he had been professor of obstetrics at Queen's and first dean of Kingston Women's Medical College. He had just been appointed warden of the penitentiary in January 1885. Reception of this choice bit of patronage should have made him grateful to the government.[8]

But Lavell alone was politically impossible; the commission had to be balanced with a French-Canadian. Macdonald's eye fell upon Doctor F.-X. Valade of Ottawa. François-Xavier Valade, then thirty-eight years old, had been born in Montreal but had set up a medical practice in Ottawa. He appears to have been politically connected to Sir Adolphe Caron, minister of militia. In 1884 Valade received an appointment as public analyst for the Department of Inland Revenue. In addition to his medical earnings, he made more than $1,000 a year testing food samples for adulteration. Like Lavell, he had no special expertise in problems of insanity, and he did not claim to be an alienist.[9]

Macdonald thus succeeded in balancing his inquiry between French and English, but the balance was more apparent than real. Valade and Lavell each received identical letters of instruction from the prime minister, telling them in effect to judge Riel by the McNaghten criterion of whether he could tell the difference between right and wrong; but Lavell received an additional letter which makes illuminating reading. Sir John wrote re Valade: "I have told him that as surgeon and warden of the P[enitentiary] you had under your charge Criminal Lunatics & were therefore an Expert. I have fully impressed him with this idea. So don't be too modest about it." (Lavell's medical specialty was obstetrics.) On the conduct of the inquiry, Sir John suggested that Lavell talk to those who knew Riel; but "I should suggest as few as possible — [stop] so soon as you are convinced that Riel knows right from wrong and is an accountable being." Finally, the prime minister added that "should you wish to inform me of anything separately from Dr. Valade Dewdney will manage that for you."[10] Obviously, Valade was to be a junior partner in this enterprise, and the prime minister was relying on Lavell to ensure that things turned out as planned. All in all, it is hard to disagree with the verdict of George Stanley that the commission was "a meaningless political sop."[11]

Because of later confusion surrounding their activities, it is necessary to describe precisely how Drs. Lavell and Valade carried out their instructions. Proceeding to Regina by separate trains, they checked into their hotels under assumed names and began their inquiry on 7 November. One aspect of their charge was to talk to those who had been with Riel in the past months — NWMP officers; Father André, his spiritual director; and Dr. Augustus Jukes, the NWMP surgeon who was attending Riel and who had already testified on behalf of the prosecution at the trial.

Dr. Jukes, in fact, functioned as a quasi-colleague of Lavell and Valade, for the prime minister also asked him to submit an opinion. On 6 November, before seeing the two eastern doctors, Jukes wrote a ten-page report to the prime minister, the essence of which was that Riel, while holding unusual views and subject to hallucinations, was legally accountable for his actions.

> I cannot escape the conviction, that except upon certain questions of a purely religious and private nature, having relation to what may be called Divine mysteries, he is perfectly sane and accountable for his actions.
> That Riel differs systematically from the large majority of mankind in the views he entertains respecting certain questions relating to religious subjects or rather to certain spiritual phenomena such as inspiration, and prophetic vision in relation thereto, must be admitted. On these subjects he cherishes illusions or hallucinations which vary materially in intensity under varying physical and mental conditions; but diversities of opinion and belief upon these and kindred subjects do not properly constitute insanity, nor do they ... interfere with or obscure in the slightest degree a clear perception of duty, or the difference between moral right and wrong ... or render his judgment less sound in the affairs of every-day life.[12]

Interestingly, Jukes added that Riel, having heard that a medical commission would examine him, welcomed the inquiry as a way to vindicate his sanity!

Jukes gave his report to Governor Dewdney who mailed it to Macdonald on the next day, simultaneously sending a telegram: "Doctors arrived this morning. Jukes' report which is long mailed last night states Riel perfectly accountable for his actions."[13] But Jukes, who had developed an affection for Riel and who disliked the idea of capital punishment, was not finished. On 9 November he wrote an even longer letter to the prime minister to suggest that a commission be established to analyze Riel's writings, to see if they stemmed from a sane or insane mind.[14] He obviously did not want Riel's blood on his hands.

Both alone and together, Lavell and Valade proceeded to examine the prisoner. They did not reveal their identity to him, telling him they were travelers who wished to make his acquaintance. At the end of two days, the doctors met to try to thrash out a report. Lavell wrote that Valade

> was at first strong for reporting Riel as of insane mind on account of his foolish expressions. I contested this with him until the last moment, pointed out as strongly as I could the defects in his conclusions, and even got admission that even in his delusions he was not really insane. But I am morally certain he [Valade] was too much in the company of Père André, and to some extent influenced. He said he could not give a report that would be decidedly adverse.[15]

In the end, the two men wrote out separate short statements for Governor Dewdney, who immediately telegraphed them to Sir John. The key sentence in Lavell's view was: "I am of opinion that Riel, although holding foolish and peculiar views concerning visions as to religion and general government, is an accountable being and knows right from wrong."[16] Valade, on the other hand, concluded:

> After having examined carefully Riel in private conversation with him and by testimony of persons who take care of him, I have come to the conclusion that he is not an accountable being, that he is unable to distinguish between right and wrong on political and religious subjects which I consider well marked typical forms of a kind of insanity under which he undoubtedly suffers, but on other points I believe him to be quite sensible and can distinguish right from wrong.[17]

After sending a telegram incorporating the text of both opinions, Dewdney immediately mailed the originals to the prime minister, together with his own assessment that the difference between the reports was only "a little difficulty about the phraseology between the two doctors."[18] But in fact Lavell and Valade, on the only issue of practical importance, had come to exactly opposite conclusions. The two doctors agreed that Riel's mind was strangely divided, and that he was completely normal on all topics except politics and religion; but they disagreed on the essential question of whether he was an "accountable being." And this was the whole issue: if he was accountable he should hang; if not, he should be sent to an asylum for the insane.

Dr. Valade left Regina that very day, and Dr. Lavell on the next; but their work was not entirely over. Before his departure from Regina, Lavell wrote Sir John a long letter recounting his experiences, and added at the end: "I will have to meet Dr. Valade at all events, to try to be able to present a joint report."[19] Apparently both men considered their telegraphed reports to be only preliminary statements, and wished to produce a more finished document, with agreement on the wording if possible.

But the prime minister was determined to move quickly without waiting for polished reports. After he had received Dewdney's telegrams giving the opinion of Jukes, Lavell, and Valade, but before he had received anything through the mails, Sir John prepared a memo for cabinet which included the text of his original letters to Valade and Lavell (though not the private instructions to Lavell) plus an accurate rendition of Dewdney's telegrams.[20] In spite of Valade's declaration that Riel was not accountable, the cabinet decided for hanging; and the French ministers, after some hesitation, supported their English colleagues. By 12 November all was settled. The point of interest here is the casual way in which the work of the medical men was treated. The cabinet was apparently satisfied with the telegraphic reports from Dewdney. They did not wait to see the original letters of the three doctors; nor did they get a chance to read Jukes's second letter which recommended further study of Riel's writings; and least of all did they wait for a considered report from Lavell and Valade. This only goes to show that the three doctors did not constitute a "commission" in the conventional sense. They were appointed in secrecy and the public learned of their mission only through a press leak; each received different instructions; they were under no obligation to prepare a joint report; each doctor was in some respect an employee of or dependent upon the federal government; and none was an expert in the field of inquiry. The doctors were only pawns in the game of political chess. Macdonald manipulated them to stiffen the resolve of his wavering French ministers.

But in spite of the prime minister's efforts to manage the outcome of the inquiry and his tactical success in holding the cabinet together, there was one untidy and embarrassing detail. Dr. Valade had written that Riel was not an accountable being. The cabinet had managed to persuade itself that Lavell and Valade meant the same thing, even if they had used different words — but what would an outsider think upon reading the telegrams? The episode could not be kept confidential because the press had learned of the doctors' errand to Regina. The papers were full of speculations about what Jukes, Lavell, and Valade had reported.

Although he had insisted on giving his opinion that Riel was not an accountable being, Dr. Valade did not feel obliged to make this public after the execution. When questioned on 20 November by an Ottawa newspaper, he said:

> It doesn't often happen that I am questioned by journalists on professional matters. Any opinion that I can express as a doctor on the Riel question should be a written opinion which will be given to the competent authorities, who, I have no doubt, will make it public in due time.[21]

This suggests that he had not lost faith in the government even though they had not seen fit to take his advice. It also suggests that he had not yet written his definitive report.

But if Valade did not want to embarrass the government, there were others of less kindly intention. In Regina, A.-E. Forget, clerk of the North-West Council and secretary to Governor Dewdney, resented Riel's execution. Because of his position, he must have had inside information about the "lunacy commission." On 23 November, Forget wrote to Honoré Mercier:

> We are certain here that Dr. Lavell admitted in his telegram to Sir John that poor Riel was touched with madness, but that he was nevertheless responsible for his actions. Dr. Valade, on the contrary, declared him completely insane and unable to distinguish between good and evil.[22]

This letter was passed on to Edward Blake, Liberal leader in the House of Commons. When the House opened in February 1886, the critics of Riel's execution were ready to press the government for disclosure of the medical reports on his accountability.

On 1 March, Sir John was asked if he would lay the reports before the House; and the prime minister, who certainly knew this was coming, readily agreed. But the documents, when they were tabled by Hector Langevin on 9 March, were not an accurate transcript of what had been received by the prime minister. A short excerpt from Jukes's letter of 6 November was included, even though at the time of the decision on 12 November Jukes's views were known to the cabinet only through Dewdney's one-sentence, telegraphic description. Jukes's letter now was conveniently condensed so as to eliminate his long descriptions of Riel's eccentricities. Dr. Lavell's telegram of 8 November was released by the government without editing — there was, after all, no need for alterations. But Dr. Valade's telegram was given to the Commons in a new version.[23]

Dr. Valade to Sir John A. Macdonald.

Regina, N.W.T., 8th November, 1885, Sir, — After having examined carefully Riel in private conversation with him and by testimony of persons who take care of him I have come to the conclusion that he suffers under hallucinations on political and religious subjects, but on other points I believe him to be quite sensible and can distinguish right from wrong.

F.X. Valade, M.D.

Comparison with the original shows that the words

that he is not an accountable being, that he is unable to distinguish between right and wrong on political and religious subjects which I consider well marked typical forms of a kind of insanity under which he undoubtedly suffers

had been replaced by the much weaker statement "that he suffers under hallucinations on political and religious subjects." This alteration took away all the embarrassing language from the telegram, which had originally found Riel not responsible for a political crime. Donald Creighton has called this "not an unfair exercise in condensation,"[24] but is it not forgery, even if done for *raison d'état?*

Behind this relatively crude forgery one can glimpse a more sophisticated attempt at manipulation of the doctors' reports. Valade and Lavell, it will be remembered, had not been able to agree on the wording of a joint report in Regina: hence the decision to send separate telegrams. But it was still hoped that the two doctors might be able, after sufficient discussion, to affix their signatures to a common document. Adolphe Caron, Valade's friend, was deputized by the prime minister to bring the two doctors together. But Caron, either on Macdonald's instructions or on his own initiative, proposed not only to encourage Valade and Lavell to reach agreement but to take a hand in the actual composition. Words can hardly describe the ludicrous spectacle of a minister of the Crown helping to write a supposedly independent report on the sanity of a man, already executed, whose fate was supposed to have been decided by the cabinet on the basis of that report.

Lavell, for his part, was only too eager to cooperate. He wrote to Caron on 14 December 1885, in a letter marked "private":

As you directed, I forward you draft copy of "Report" from my stand point of the case. It at all events gives my own view, and I hope will meet my colleague's [Valade's]. I shall be glad to have the honour of your own views as to points which ought to be excluded, or added. It is of importance, I know, that it should bear criticism, and I will be quite willing to bear my full share regarding the opinions expressed. There may be some matters of policy requiring some changes on which I would like your judgment.[25]

With this letter, Lavell included an eleven-page draft of a joint report, written in a "we" style throughout and dated 9 November 1885.[26] It contained a longer exposition of the view which Lavell had summarized in his telegram to the prime minister, namely that Riel was sane, accountable for his acts, and fit to be executed. Valade perhaps had seen and rejected this document in Regina; he certainly was familiar with, and partially disagreed with, Lavell's judgment on the question of accountability.

For unknown reasons, Caron's attempt at intervention and mediation did not succeed. Failing to secure a politically acceptable report, the cabinet then resorted to forgery to conceal, or at least disguise, Valade's original opinion.

In the House of Commons the Liberals, sensing that something was amiss, pressed for the production of the original documents. On 15 March, Sir John Thompson, minister of justice, rose to explain why the original letters could not be produced. He said, truthfully enough, that the cabinet had acted on the basis of telegrams, whereas what had been tabled on 9 March had been compiled from the letters received later. He went on to say that the telegrams could not be tabled because they were no longer in possession of the government, having been returned to the senders once the letters were received. This latter statement, if true, certainly represents an unusual philosophy of record-keeping; but it was in any event irrelevant to the real question of whether the government had accurately reproduced the original reports, either written or telegraphic. By introducing this irrelevancy into the debate, Thompson succeeded in blunting the opposition's attack. Blake fulminated that "we have here cooked-up documents,"[27] but he could not prove anything without hard evidence, which was not in his possession. In the face of the government's stonewalling, the only proof could come from Valade himself; and the doctor, for reasons which can only be conjectured, kept silent. Perhaps he was bribed or threatened with loss of his position as public analyst.[28] But more likely is that, like many French Canadians who retained their loyalty to the government, he felt that the country had suffered enough over Riel, and that it was best to bring the debate to an end. He could tell himself that he had done his duty as a physician, and the rest was in the hands of the politicians — not his business.

However, he did take one further step in private. Sometime in late 1885 or early 1886, having failed to agree on a joint statement with Dr. Lavell, he wrote his own report. It is not known whether this lengthy memorandum (thirty-five manuscript pages) was actually submitted to the prime minister. All that survives is a letterpress copy kept by Valade that was later given by his family to the Public Archives of Canada.[29]

The text gave a description of Riel's behavior and prophetic claims which matched the accounts of Jukes and Lavell, but Valade's interpretation differed from that of his colleagues. Whereas they had argued on the basis of the cognitive test established in the McNaghten Rules, Valade resorted to the concept of monomania developed by the pioneering French alienists Pinel and Esquirol. "Monomania," says a modern historian, purported to be "insanity focussed on one area of perception or action, in some cases accompanied by extensive lucid periods."[30] This was how Valade saw Riel:

> We have observed and discovered in the conversation and conduct of the prisoner Riel the evidence of fixed delusions, the expressions of which could by no logical sequence be linked on to ideas previously expressed. It is of no consequence that he manifested lucid intervals, and that he could even talk like a philosopher; nor is it of any importance that taking his fixed delusion as a starting point, he could reason logically in that direction; this would only go to prove that the reasoning faculty was not entirely destroyed. A railway train running off the track keeps going for some time.[31]

Such a conception of mental alienation was volitional, not cognitive. Even though Riel knew what he was doing in an abstract sense, and realized that it violated the law, he could not stop himself. Thus Valade decided:

> In conclusion we may state that for the advocates of partial responsibility there exists in the monomaniac two distinct personalities, the one sane, the other insane: now the latter alone is not answerable for his acts, since he has been pushed to commit them by a hallucination, a delirious conception or a delusion.
>
> I have stated that Louis Riel was suffering from political-religious hallucinations but on all other matters, he was responsible for his acts, and could distinguish right from wrong. All this means and meant very clearly that in the sphere of the fixed delusions which were constantly occupying his mind and

which were the one theme of his writings, speeches, and conversations, he was not fit to perceive the crime of High Treason of which he had been guilty; and that when I examined him he could not in my humble opinion, distinguish between right and wrong on politico-religious questions.[32]

The difference between Valade on the one hand, and Jukes and Lavell on the other, was a confrontation between two outlooks. Jukes and Lavell exemplified the dominant legal view of insanity in contemporary British law. Valade represented the common opinion of alienists in Great Britain and particularly in France, where the legal doctrine was also different from the British. The French Penal Code read: "There is neither crime nor offence if the accused was in a state of mental alienation at the time of doing the act or if he was constrained by a force which he could not resist."[33]

Should the cabinet have advised the governor general to commute Riel's sentence and transfer him to a lunatic asylum? This discretionary exercise of the royal prerogative of mercy would have been theoretically possible regardless of legal doctrine. The head of state is not bound to give reasons for an act of clemency. However, as a practical matter it would have been extraordinary for the cabinet to depart from the Canadian and British approach embodied in the McNaghten Rules to rely upon the view of insanity which Valade had adopted from French sources. There is no evidence that the Riel seen by Lavell and Valade in November 1885 was much different from the man who instigated the Rebellion in March or who stood trial in July. His profound belief in his prophetic "mission" seemed to outsiders to be an irrational obsession, but no one could deny his general rationality in dealing with the affairs of life. Such a person was without doubt legally accountable for his actions under the McNaghten Rules, for he knew he was violating the law even if his obsession "made" him take legal risks.

However, if the government made a legally defensible decision in the end, its methods were less than admirable. The medical men were manipulated from start to finish in a Machiavellian way: the doctors were not truly independent of the government; there were secret instructions to one member of the commission; the cabinet acted without waiting for full reports; a minister tried to fix the reports retroactively; and a falsified document was tabled in the House of Commons. This is the one episode in the North-West Rebellion in which the government may be accused, not of delays or mistaken judgments, but of bad faith.

CHAPTER EIGHT

A POSTHUMOUS PARDON?

As students of history we may be interested in establishing the record of the past and determining how and why things happened as they did, but as human beings we also want to know who deserves praise or blame according to our ethical conceptions. Without this moral dimension, history would be little more than antiquarianism.

No easy moral judgments can be made about the North-West Rebellion. For its part, the government of Canada certainly deserves some censure. With respect to the river-lot issue much hard feeling could have been avoided if the whole settlement of St. Laurent had been surveyed at the outset according to the wishes of the *Métis*, or if a resurvey had been carried out as was ultimately done. Also, the government was wrong in procrastinating so long over the half-breed land grant in the North-West. It was praiseworthy to seek an alternative to the Manitoba grant; but when no other feasible model was found, it would have been much better to go ahead than by delay to create the fear among the North-West half-breeds that there would be no grant at all.

These are severe criticisms, but they must be kept in proper perspective. They were mistakes in judgment, not part of a calculated campaign to destroy the *Métis* or deprive them of their rights. Under political pressure, the government did implement a land grant and did adjust the river-lot claims. Government is never perfect; it is difficult to ask more of a system than that it be capable of correcting mistakes in a reasonable period of time. I believe the Canadian government's performance in these matters passed that test.

Judgments about Louis Riel are also necessarily complex. No one will deny that he was the greatest leader the *Métis* have produced and that he made the advancement of his people the overriding purpose of his life. But it is clear that he had little real concern for the issues of river lots and the land grant which had goaded the *Métis* of St. Laurent into seeking his help. For him, these were only stepping stones to his vast scheme of a new settlement of aboriginal claims. To that extent, he might be accused of using his followers as pawns in his own game. It is also beyond dispute that Riel was pursuing a private strategy of getting money from the government and that this sometimes took precedence over his efforts on behalf of the *Métis*.

As regards the aftermath of the Rebellion, the evidence shows that Riel's trial was as procedurally fair as was obtainable within the limitations of the Territorial courts. There was a rational argument for the cabinet to commute the death sentence to a lesser penalty; but this was a matter of discretion, not of right, and there were also strong arguments for letting the sentence be carried out. The only way in which the government acted improperly was in its manipulation of the medical commission — admittedly a shameful episode.

Does all of this justify a posthumous pardon for Riel, as demanded in 1979 by the Association of Métis and Non-Status Indians of Saskatchewan? The conclusion of their brief to the cabinet is worth quoting at length for the way it summarizes many current beliefs:

> We, therefore, request on behalf of all the Métis people and on behalf of others who look to Riel's example for inspiration, that the Canadian Government act immediately by exercising the Royal Prerogative of mercy and by conveying to the Métis organization a grant of pardon for Riel. . . . the government clearly has the authority to take such action. Although we know of no historical precedent in Canada for a posthumous pardon, the Imperial Parliament of Britain has provided the mechanism for it. The arguments in favour of such action are strong.
>
> a) Riel acted out of the conviction that he was right in International Law to advocate the recognition of the rights of his people;
> b) Riel did not act for reasons of personal gain or to enhance his own reputation;
> c) Riel himself committed no illegal act either at the Red River or at Batoche;
> d) Riel did not advocate war or armed resistance and only armed his people to enable them to protect themselves in the face of what they believed were hostile intentions towards them by the government;
> e) The government could have avoided the violence and

destruction by having indicated some preparedness to recognize the legitimate rights of the people and to negotiate a settlement;

f) When the violence did occur, it happened more by accident than as a result of any deliberate plan by Riel to have his people rise in armed revolt;

g) Riel consistently avoided using available military strategy to take advantage of government police and troops;

h) Riel did not receive a fair trial because of bias and prejudice toward him from many quarters;

i) The government ignored the jury's recommendation of mercy;

j) The government by such action today could renew the faith of the Métis people in the possibility of just treatment for themselves within Canadian society. This is especially important during the current movement for National Unity.[1]

This proposal requires serious thought. Although it was not acted upon when it was first made and it is not under consideration by government at the present moment, it is likely to be revived with the backing of many Métis organizations at the time of the centennial of the North-West Rebellion. It is worth considering the merits of the question now so as not to be carried away in a flood of sentiment in 1985.

Probably all legal systems have some provision for the exercise of clemency in cases where erroneous convictions have occurred or where special circumstances call for mitigation of legally prescribed punishment. The authority to grant clemency is usually vested in the chief executive of the state, and sometimes in the legislative assembly as well.[2] In the British tradition, the royal prerogative of mercy is part of the broad prerogative powers of the Crown. The king or queen has always had the right to commute sentences or grant pardons, even without any statutory authority from Parliament. This power is transferred to the governor general of Canada through the Letters Patent which constitute that office. In the early days of Confederation, the governor general exercised this power on his own initiative, as when Lord Dufferin in 1875 reduced Ambroise Lépine's death sentence to two years imprisonment and forfeiture of political rights. Today it would be considered unconstitutional for the governor general to exercise the royal prerogative of mercy under the Letters Patent except on the advice of the cabinet.

The Parliament of Canada has also created another way of granting pardons. Section 683(2) of the Criminal Code states: "The Governor in Council may grant a free pardon or a conditional pardon to any person who has been convicted of an offense."³ The phrase "Governor in Council" means in effect the cabinet meeting as a body. In practice, applications for pardon are handled by the solicitor general's office, which refers them to the National Parole Board for advice. Although the cabinet must review the Parole Board's recommendation, it does not normally deliberate on the facts of particular cases. However, in a case like Riel's where the purpose of a pardon would be to make a political statement, the cabinet would undoubtedly discuss the matter in some depth.

Most applications for the royal prerogative of mercy are now processed under the Criminal Code rather than under the Letters Patent. However, the latter procedure is still alive, for section 686 of the Criminal Code states: "Nothing in this Act in any manner limits or affects Her Majesty's royal prerogative of mercy."⁴ In 1978-79, sixty applications were processed under the Criminal Code, twelve under the Letters Patent.⁵ Because of the ceremonial and symbolic value of the office of governor general, it is likely that the government would prefer this route if it wished to act in Riel's case.

There does not seem to be any legal barrier to granting a pardon posthumously. I know of no Canadian precedent, but in Britain in 1967 the queen pardoned one Timothy Evans, who had been hanged in 1950 for the murder of his child. An inquiry in the interim had pointed to Mr. Evans's innocence.⁶ This British case is presumably a valid precedent for Canada. Responding to an inquiry in 1981, a spokesman for the National Parole Board saw no obstacle to a posthumous pardon under either the Letters Patent or the Criminal Code.⁷

What is the meaning of a pardon? Does it utterly blot out guilt, or does it merely remove the punishment attached to guilt? The Supreme Court of the United States said in a famous case:

> A pardon reaches both the punishment prescribed for the offense and the guilt of the offender. . . . It releases the punishment and blots out of existence the guilt, so that in the eye of the law the offender is as innocent as if he had never committed the offense. . . . It makes him, as it were, a new man, and gives him a new credit and capacity.⁸

Although these words have often been cited in subsequent cases, there are many other precedents which assert that a pardon only removes punishment but does not absolve guilt. Considered in the abstract, the meaning of a pardon is ambiguous.

However, this ambiguity need not exist in Canada, for our government grants both "free" and "ordinary" pardons. Free pardons are granted in instances where subsequent investigation shows erroneous conviction. In such cases, justice demands restoration of the reputation of one who was innocent of wrong-doing. Thus the governor general might emit a document reading as follows:

> Now therefore know ye that We, considering that you, the said John Doe, being innocent of the said alleged offence of which you were convicted as aforesaid, should no longer remain subject to the operation or stigma of the aforesaid conviction and sentence, Have pardoned and Released you, and We Do hereby Grant into you a Free Pardon and Remission in respect thereof . . .[9]

An ordinary pardon is granted where an offender's guilt is not in doubt but where circumstances make further punishment ill-advised. In such cases the document might read:

> Now therefore know ye that having taken the premises into consideration, and for divers good causes we thereinto moving, being willing to extend the Royal clemency unto him, the said John Doe, I have pardoned, remitted and released him, the said John Doe, of and from the said conviction and of and from all and every the penalties to which the said John Doe was and is liable in pursuance thereof.[10]

In the light of this book, it is clear that a pardon for Riel could only be an ordinary, not a free pardon. There is no reason to believe that his trial was unfair or that he did not commit the actions of which he was accused. Governmental errors in policy or administration, real though they may have been, could not be a legal justification for waging war against the sovereign. This point is so essential that I would rather see no pardon at all for Riel than a free pardon, for the latter would create utterly false impressions about Canadian justice in the nineteenth century.

Obviously, the value of any posthumous pardon is symbolic; the death sentence cannot be remitted once it is carried out. Hence it is vital to look at the symbolism of a posthumous pardon to see what message would be conveyed. A free pardon, because it would carry the false message that Riel did not break the law, is unacceptable. But the message of an ordinary pardon would be that there were circumstances which helped to explain the Rebellion and that the government itself was not wholly blameless. This is undoubtedly what Riel's jury meant when it convicted him of high treason but asked the foreman "to recommend the prisoner to the mercy of the

Crown."[11] The judge could not legally respond to this request in passing sentence, but it was always open to the government to reduce the sentence in some way. Such a decision is a matter of policy based upon assessment of all relevant circumstances. That the cabinet found it impolitic in 1885 to extend clemency does not preclude it from doing so as a symbolic gesture in 1985.

Riel's offense of high treason was a political crime, that is, an offense against the state, an attempt to overthrow constitutional government in favor of a new power. He may not have intended this when he first took hostages and cut telegraph lines, but the armed confrontation with the Mounted Police and his attempts to create a mass rising turned breach of the peace into treason. Now political crimes are paradoxical. In one sense, they are perceived as the gravest of all offenses because they threaten the community's definition of itself, symbolized in the authority of the sovereign. Yet political offenses are more frequently pardoned than other crimes, and for two reasons.

First, they are generally committed out of adherence to principle rather than mere passion or desire for individual gain. A community which values political principle respects commitment to principle even when it conflicts with the beliefs of the majority or the dominant principles of the state. Extending clemency is a way of showing that the political offender is not simply in the same class with common criminals. Liberal democracies are especially inclined to show mercy to political offenders, but even authoritarian or totalitarian regimes sometimes amnesty the wretched political prisoners who fill their jails. Clemency for the political criminal is a gesture based on strength. It is a way of saying that the government is so secure in the people's allegiance that it can afford to be merciful even to those who would challenge the constitution.

Second, most political crimes, except for individual espionage, have an important social dimension. Riel was not alone in defying Canada. He led hundreds of followers who fought till they had nothing left to fire from their rifles but stones and scrap metal. As Edmund Burke said in another context, "I do not know the method of drawing up an indictment against a whole people."[12] History made Riel the leader of the Métis people during his life and their symbol after his death. The government did in fact show considerable leniency to the Métis after the Rebellion; not many were prosecuted, no one except Riel was sentenced to death, and indeed no one served more than a year in prison. A posthumous pardon for Riel would confirm at the symbolic level the clemency already shown at the practical level.

The historical record of Western governments in extending clemency for political crimes is mixed. There are many cases where the full sentence was exacted in strict justice, as in the execution by the British of the leaders of the Easter uprising in Dublin, 1916. Severity is especially likely when, as in that case, the government is locked in a major war. But there are also many examples of mercy to cite as precedents. No leaders of the Confederacy were hanged or even prosecuted after the American Civil War; they were treated more like defeated adversaries than like traitors.[13] In Canada, some were hanged after the rebellion of 1837, but those such as George Cartier and Louis-Joseph Papineau who fled to the United States were later allowed to return to the country and resume their political careers. Four *patriotes* even went on to become prime ministers of the united province of Canada.[14] If there is a general rule, it is that clemency is extended when the authorities feel that the public order is secure and withheld when insurrection still seems a real possibility.

These arguments present a superficially plausible case for granting Riel a posthumous ordinary pardon as a gesture of reconciliation toward Canada's native peoples. However, my own opinion is that such a pardon would be a mistake. If history is not to be falsified, the government will have to stress that this is an ordinary, not a free pardon, which does not establish Riel's innocence. But a gesture of this type is not likely to be seen by the Métis as a genuine act of clemency. Since Riel is dead, an ordinary pardon cannot have its normal effect of remitting punishment; and since Métis organizations are vociferous in maintaining Riel's innocence, they will not like the symbolic message of an ordinary pardon. They may well condemn it as another cynical ploy by the government, and the outcome may be the exact opposite of the intended reconciliation. To avoid this confrontation, it would be necessary to issue a free pardon, or perhaps an ordinary pardon accompanied by publicity which played down the difference between the two kinds of pardon. But this course of action would contradict all the research presented in this book. It would strengthen the already common misconceptions that the government acted unjustly toward the *Métis*, that Riel had no alternative but violence, and that he did not receive a fair trial. I conclude that we should leave history as it is. The tragedy of the Rebellion cannot be effaced by a sentimental gesture one hundred years later. We can pay better tribute to the men of 1885 by close study of the irreversible events in which they took part. Their losses will not have been in vain if we can learn to avoid similar mistakes in the future.

NOTES

PREFACE

1. Thomas Flanagan, ed., *The Diaries of Louis Riel* (Edmonton: Hurtig, 1976); Gilles Martel, Glen Campbell, Thomas Flanagan, *Louis Riel: Poésies de Jeunesse* (St. Boniface: Les Editions du Blé, 1977).
2. Thomas Flanagan, *Louis "David" Riel: "Prophet of the New World"* (Toronto: University of Toronto Press, 1979).
3. G. F. G. Stanley et al., "The Collected Writings of Louis Riel/Les Ecrits Complets de Louis Riel" (Edmonton: University of Alberta Press, 1985; 5 volumes). Forthcoming.

CHAPTER ONE

1. For a full historical account of the North-West Rebellion, see George F. G. Stanley, *The Birth of Western Canada* (Toronto: University of Toronto Press, 1963; first published 1936); Desmond Morton, *The Last War Drum* (Toronto: Hakkert, 1972).
2. Gabriel Dumont & Alex Fisher to the Lieutenant-Governor of the North-West Territories, 1 February 1878, CSP (1885), 116, p. 28.
3. All printed, ibid.
4. *Le Manitoba*, 16 March 1883.
5. A badly spelled French version of the text is found in PAM, MG 3 D2, File 18, "[compte rendu d'une] Assemblée Publique tenue à St. Laurent à la Résidence d'Esidore Dumont, le 21 Avril, 1884." An English translation of the last five points of the list, lacking the first two as well as the preamble, is PAC, RG 13 B2, 48-50. In the version printed here, I have used this translation and added to it my own translation of the missing paragraphs.
6. PAC, MG 26 A, 42261-66; J.-V. Grandin, "Memorial of the grievances

given to me by Messrs. Charles Nolin and Maxime Lépine . . . ,"
English translation of French original sent by Grandin to the prime
minister, 13 June 1884.

7. Donald Creighton, *John A. Macdonald: The Old Chieftain* (Toronto:
    Macmillan of Canada, 1955), ch. 12.

8. See his account in Adolphe Ouimet, ed., *La Vérité sur la question métisse
    au Nord-Ouest* (Montréal: B.A.T. de Montigny, 1889), p. 117.

9. A.-H. de Trémaudan, *Histoire de la nation métisse dans l'Ouest canadien*
    (Montréal: Editions Albert Lévesque, 1936); tr. Elizabeth Maguet, *Hold
    High Your Heads* (Winnipeg: Pemmican Publications, 1982).

10. Howard Adams, *Prison of Grass* (Toronto: New Press, 1975).

11. Stanley, *Birth of Western Canada*, pp. 261, 314.

12. Joseph K. Howard, *Strange Empire: Louis Riel and the Métis People* (first
    published 1957; Toronto: James Lewis and Samuel, 1974), pp.
    371-373; Robert E. Lamb, *Thunder in the North* (New York: Pageant
    Press, 1957), pp. 125-127; E. B. Osler, *The Man Who Had to Hang: Louis
    Riel* (Toronto: Longmans, 1961), pp. 224-227; Peter Charlebois, *The
    Life of Louis Riel* (Toronto: NC Press, 1975), pp. 131 ff.

13. The psychiatric literature on Riel is listed in Flanagan, *Louis "David"
    Riel*, p. 187.

14. George F. G. Stanley, *Louis Riel* (Toronto: Ryerson, 1963).

15. Desmond Morton, ed., *The Queen v Louis Riel* (Toronto: University of
    Toronto Press, 1974), pp. xxii, xxx.

16. George Manuel and Michael Posluns, *The Fourth World* (Don Mills:
    Collier Macmillan, 1974).

17. Association of Métis and Non-Status Indians of Saskatchewan, *Louis
    Riel: Justice Must be Done* (Winnipeg: Manitoba Métis Federation Press,
    1979).

18. For an interim report on the Louis Riel Project, see Thomas Flanagan
    and Claude Rocan, "A Guide to the Louis Riel Papers," *Archivaria* 11
    (Winter, 1980-81): 135-69.

19. See Thérèse-E. Lafontaine, "Louis Riel: A Preliminary Bibliography
    1963-1978," in A. S. Lussier, ed., *Riel and the Métis* (Winnipeg,
    Manitoba: Manitoba Métis Federation Press, 1979), pp. 161-200.

CHAPTER TWO

1. I have relied in general on Chester Martin, *"Dominion Lands" Policy*
    (Toronto: Macmillan, 1938); Courtney C. J. Bond, *Surveyors of Canada*
    (Ottawa: Canadian Institute of Surveying, 1966), pp. 19-31; Don W.
    Thomson, *Men and Meridians* (Ottawa: Queen's Printer, 1967), II, pp.
    26-59.

2. Compiled from annual reports of the Department of the Interior in the
    Canadian Sessional Papers, 1880-85. Hereafter cit. as *CSP*.

3. André Lalonde, "Colonization Companies in the 1880's," *Saskatchewan
    History* 24 (1971): 101-14.

4. UAA, William Pearce Papers, MG 9/2/6/4/9, folder 885, "Lands
    Obtained under the Manitoba Act in Manitoba, and Surveys
    Incidental to the Granting of Titles Therefor," 15 December 1913.

5.   D. N. Sprague is the only scholar to have made a close study of the river lot question in Manitoba. In the following discussion, I have drawn on his articles "Government Lawlessness in the Administration of Manitoba Land Claims, 1830–1885," *Manitoba Law Journal* 10 (1980): 415–41; and "The Manitoba Land Question," *Journal of Canadian Studies* 15 (1980): 74–84.

6.   The Manitoba Act, 33 Vict., c.3, s.32.

7.   Sprague, "Government Lawlessness," 440.

8.   S.C. 1874, c.20, s.3.

9.   UAA, William Pearce Papers, file 459, "Titles to Land: Early Administration and Development," n.d., pp. 26–29.

10.   See the annual reports of the Department of the Interior, *CSP* (1878), No. 10, p. xxiv, and *CSP* (1882), No. 18, p. 2.

11.   See the articles by Sprague cited *supra*, note 5.

12.   Nancy L. Woolworth, "Gingras, St. Joseph, and the Métis in the Northern Red River Valley," *North Dakota History* 42 (1975): 16–23.

13.   I have not found a copy of these instructions to surveyors regarding river lots, but have inferred them from the evidence of what was done in the field. Standing orders are mentioned in E. De Ville to A. M. Burgess, 26 November 1883, *CSP* (1885), No. 116, p. 54.

14.   The calculations will be found in the annual report of the Department of the Interior, *CSP* (1877), No. 11, p. 35.

15.   Gary W. D. Abrams, *Prince Albert: The First Century 1866–1966* (Saskatoon: Modern Press, 1966), pp. 1–33.

16.   Diane Payment, *Structural and Settlement History of Batoche Village* (Parks Canada, Manuscript Report No. 248, 1977), 15–19; A. André, "La Petite Chronique de St-Laurent," entry of 12 May 1872, PAA, Oblate Papers, D-IV-125.

17.   A. André, "La Petite Chronique de St-Laurent," 1878.

18.   A. L. Russell to Lindsay Russell, 24 November 1877; Department of the Interior, annual report 1877, *CSP* (1878), No. 10, pp. 13–14.

19.   Petition to the minister of the interior, 15 January 1878; *CSP* (1885), No. 116, p. 24.

20.   Petition to the governor general in council, n.d.; *CSP* (1885), No. 116, p. 29.

21.   Petition to the lieutenant-governor of the N.W.T., 1 February 1878; ibid., p. 28.

22.   Montague Aldous to Lindsay Russell, 13 November 1878; Department of the Interior, annual report 1878, *CSP* (1879), No. 7, App. 6, p. 23.

23.   Ibid., p. 24.

24.   Dates of surveys are taken from township plans.

25.   William Pearce to Thomas White, 14 December 1885, in "All Claims to Land and Right to Participate in the North-West Half-Breed Grant by Settlers along the South Saskatchewan and Vicinity," *CSP* (1886), No. 8b, p. 2.

26.   Ibid.

27.   Edgar Dewdney to J. A. Macdonald, 9 September 1884; PAC, RG 10, Black Series, file 15446.

28.   A. André to the lieutenant-governor in council, n.d.; *CSP* (1885), No. 116, p. 98.
29.   Lawrence Clarke to the lieutenant-governor in council, 7 June 1881; ibid., p. 97.
30.   A. Russell to George Duck, 2 August 1881; ibid., p. 96. The date of 21 September 1881, is given by William Pearce in his report of his investigation of Prince Albert land claims, PAC, RG 15, file 65366.
31.   Lloyd Rodwell, "Land Claims in the Prince Albert Settlement," *Saskatchewan History* 19 (1966): 1–23; "Prince Albert River Lots," ibid 19 (1966): 100–110.
32.   There are two reports of this meeting, one by Thomas McKay, chairman, *CSP* (1885), No. 116, pp. 69–70, and one by H. MacBeath, secretary, ibid., pp. 73–74.
33.   Lindsay Russell to Lawrence Clarke, 22 November 1881; ibid., p. 73.
34.   PAC, RG 15, file 44719. The undated memorial was printed for distribution.
35.   J. A. Macdonald to David Macpherson, 7 July 1882, cited in E. Alyn Mitchener, "William Pearce and Federal Government Activity in Western Canada" (Ph.D. dissertation, University of Alberta, 1971), p. 85.
36.   PAC, MG 26 A, 42325. This seems to be a memo by A. M. Burgess to David Macpherson, composed April 1885, to help the minister answer criticism of the Department of the Interior. I have not found contemporary documentation of the original decision to send Russell.
37.   PAC, RG 15, file 66680.
38.   Ibid.
39.   Pearce's report, dated 12 March 1884, is in PAC, RG 15, file 65366, together with other correspondence pertaining to the investigation. It is described in Rodwell, "Land Claims in the Prince Albert Settlement."
40.   PAC, RG 15, file 65366.
41.   "La Petite Chronique de St-Laurent," 1882; PAA, Oblate Papers, D-IV-125.
42.   Ibid., year 1883.
43.   George Duck to surveyor general, 11 March 1882; *CSP* (1885), No. 116, p. 46.
44.   A. M. Burgess to George Duck, 21 September 1882, ibid.
45.   Petition to J. A. Macdonald, 4 September 1882, ibid., p. 47.
46.   Lindsay Russell to Charles Nolin, 13 October 1882; ibid., p. 48.
47.   A. André to J. A. Macdonald, 16 January 1883; ibid., pp. 54–55.
48.   D. L. Macpherson to Lindsay Russell, 23 April 1883; ibid., p. 54.
49.   *Le Manitoba*, 3 April 1883.
50.   Memorial of lieutenant-governor and council of the North-West Territories, n.d. but *ca.* Sept.–Oct. 1883, *CSP* (1885), No. 116, pp. 59–61.
51.   PAA, Oblate Papers, Codex Historicus de St-Albert 1875–1884, p. 215; Jules Le Chevallier, *Batoche* (Montréal: L'Oeuvre de Presse

Dominicaine, 1941), pp. 19–24; *Le Manitoba*, 27 February 1883; speech by Edward Blake, 6 July 1885, *House of Commons Debates*, 3105–06.

52. A. André, "La Petite Chronique de St-Laurent," 1883; PAA, Oblate Papers, D–IV–125.
53. Petition, 19 November 1883; *CSP* (1885), No. 116, p. 67.
54. Louis Schmidt to George Duck, 9 December 1883; ibid., p. 66.
55. Payment, *Structural and Settlement History*, pp. 98–99.
56. Pearce, "All Claims to Land," p. 2.
57. William Pearce to the minister of the interior, 17 January 1884; *CSP* (1885), No. 116, p. 66.
58. E.g., William Pearce to the minister of the interior, 19 March 1884; ibid., pp. 62–63.
59. V. Végréville to E. De Ville, 19 January 1884; ibid., pp. 64–65.
60. E. De Ville to A. M. Burgess, 14 February 1884; ibid., pp. 63–64.
61. John Hull to E. De Ville, 10 March 1884; ibid., p. 63.
62. William Pearce to the minister of the interior, 19 March 1884; ibid., pp. 62–63.
63. William Pearce to A. M. Burgess, 26 January 1884; PAC, RG 15, file 69266. Telegrams and correspondence relative to Pearce's decision not to go to St. Laurent are in ibid., file 65366.
64. Seventy-eight of the affidavits collected by Duck are in SAB(S), Homestead Files, 81184. The earliest are dated 2 May 1884.
65. Louis Schmidt to the minister of the interior, 26 April 1884; *CSP* (1885), No. 116, pp. 61–62.
66. Vital Grandin to J. A. Macdonald, 13 June 1884; PAC, MG 26 A, 42257–66 (English translation).
67. The interpretation of Pearce in his letter to A. M. Burgess, 26 January 1886; PAC, RG 15, file 69266.
68. The figure of ninety-nine is taken from a sheet of paper in the Macdonald Papers which seems to belong with the schedule prepared by Duck, PAC, MG 26 A, 42375. The schedule itself has not been found.
69. George Duck to A. Walsh, Commissioner of Dominion Lands, 17 June 1884; PAC, RG 15, file 84478.
70. Ibid.
71. Pearce, "All Claims to Land," p. 3; William Pearce to A. M. Burgess, 31 October, 1884, in the Annual Report of the Department of the Interior for 1884, *CSP* (1885), No. 13, p. 14.
72. Mitchener, "William Pearce and Federal Government Activity," pp. 74–108.
73. John McTaggart, Prince Albert Lands Agent, to the commissioner of Dominion Lands, 25 February 1885; PAC, RG 15, file 69266.
74. Pearce, "All Claims to Land," p. 3. Copies of these letters have not been found, but the dates given by Pearce are verified by entries in many of the relevant files in SAB(S), Homestead Files.
75. A. André to George Duck, 23 December 1885; PAC, RG 15, file 84478.
76. SAB(S), Homestead Files 81184, 205321.

77. Ibid., 81184, 889913.
78. See the correspondence in PAC, RG 10, Black series, file 15446.
79. Pearce, "All Claims to Land," p. 2.
80. P. B. Douglas to commissioner of Dominion Lands, 18 March 1885; PAC, RG 15, file 69266.
81. Report of 29 October 1885, ibid.
82. Ibid.; Pearce, "All Claims to Land," p. 17; SAB(S), Homestead Files, 121489.
83. This point is particularly vivid in the document forwarded to the prime minister by Bishop Grandin, 13 June 1884; PAC, MG 26 A, 42257-66 (English translation).
84. Payment, *Structural and Settlement History*, pp. 103-4.
85. Rodwell, "Prince Albert River Lots," 100-110.
86. SAB(S), Ag 11, files 106853, 106854.
87. SAB(S), Homestead Files, 889913.
88. PAC, RG 15, file 69266 contains an English translation of the letter of V. Végréville to E. De Ville, 19 January 1884, covered with marginal notes showing errors of fact.

CHAPTER THREE

1. Letter of instruction to delegates, 22 March 1870, cited in W. L. Morton, ed., *Alexander Begg's Red River Journal* (Toronto: Champlain Society, 1956), p. 135. Harry W. Daniels, *Native People and the Constitution of Canada* (Ottawa: Native Council of Canada, 1981), p. 56, contains a misleadingly entitled "Manitoba Bill of Rights," which purports to prove that the *Métis* of Red River were demanding a land grant as early as November 1869. But the document is wrongly identified and interpreted. It is actually a letter from John Young Bown, an Ontario M.P., to John A. Macdonald, 18 November 1869, describing the alleged demands of the half-breeds. Bown's source was probably his brother, Dr. W. R. Bown, proprietor of the *Nor'Wester* and a well-known antagonist of the *Métis* — scarcely to be considered a reliable interpreter of their true desires. PAC, MG 26 A, 40808-15.
2. W. L. Morton, ed., *Manitoba: The Birth of a Province* (Altona, Man.: Manitoba Record Society, 1965), pp. 140-43. The diary was first published in G. F. G. Stanley, "Le Journal de l'abbé N. J. Ritchot — 1870," *Revue d'Histoire de l'Amérique Française* 17 (1964): 537-64.
3. The Manitoba Act, 33 Vict., c.3, s.31 (1870).
4. N.-J. Ritchot to G.-E. Cartier, 18 May 1870. "Report of the Select Committee on the Causes of the Difficulties in the North-West Territory," *Journals of the House of Commons* (1874), Vol. 8, App. 6, p. 73.
5. An Act to Authorize Free Grants of Land to Certain Original Settlers and Their Descendents . . . , 36 Vict., c.37 (1873).
6. *House of Commons Debates*, 6 July 1885, p. 3113.
7. *House of Commons Debates*, 2 and 4 May 1870, pp. 1302 and 1359. (As

Hansard did not yet exist in 1870, this volume has been compiled from
newspaper reports of speeches.)

8.   This section is based on reading of the literature rather than my own
research in primary sources. The main secondary works are H.
Douglas Kemp, "Land Grants Under the Manitoba Act," *Transactions
of the Historical and Scientific Society of Manitoba* Series III, No. 9 (1954):
33–52; D. Bruce Sealey, *Statutory Land Rights of the Manitoba Métis*
(Winnipeg: Manitoba Métis Federation Press, 1975); idem, "Statutory
Land Rights of the Manitoba Métis," in A. S. Lussier and D. B. Sealey,
The Other Natives (Winnipeg: Manitoba Métis Federation Press, 1978),
pp. 1–30; D. N. Sprague, "The Manitoba Land Question, 1870–1882,"
Journal of Canadian Studies 15 (Fall 1980): 74–84; idem, "Government
Lawlessness in the Administration of Manitoba Land Claims, 1870-
1887," *Manitoba Law Journal* 10 (1980): 415–41; Métis Association of
Alberta, *Métis Land Rights in Alberta: A Political History* (Edmonton:
Métis Association of Alberta, 1981), pp. 87–158.

9.   Sprague, "Government Lawlessness," 417–18. I do not agree with
Sprague's view that Archibald's interpretation was the legally correct
one and that subsequent changes by the government were illegal and
unconstitutional amendments of the Manitoba Act, which, after the
B.N.A. Act of 1871 (34 and 35 Vict., c.28), could not be amended by
the Parliament of Canada.

10.   Kemp, "Land Grants," 38.

11.   An Act to Remove Doubts as to the Construction of Section 31 of the
Act 33 Victoria, Chapter 38, 36 Vict., c.38.

12.   The Half-Breed Land Grant Protection Act, S.M. 1874, c.44.

13.   An Act to Authorize Free Grants of Land to Certain Original Settlers
and Their Descendents . . . , 36 Vict., c.37.

14.   An Act Respecting the Appropriation of Certain Dominion Lands in
Manitoba, 37 Vict., c.20.

15.   A map showing the townships is in Sealey, *Statutory Land Rights of the
Manitoba Métis*, p. 80.

16.   These totals come from office consolidations of the Department of
Interior prepared by N.-O. Coté — PAC, RG 15, Vol. 227. I believe
they are the most complete figures available.

17.   Manitoba Métis Federation, *Riverlots and Scrip: Elements of Métis
Aboriginal Rights* (Winnipeg, 1978), pp. 13–25.

18.   Sealey, "Statutory Land Rights," 27.

19.   See the list of names in Emile Pelletier, *Exploitation of Métis Lands*
(Winnipeg: Manitoba Métis Federation Press, 1979; 2nd edition), pp.
23–24.

20.   Sprague, "Manitoba Land Question," 79.

21.   Sprague, "Government Lawlessness," 419–22.

22.   Sealey, "Statutory Land Rights," 24, says fifty cents an acre. Marcel
Giraud, "The Western Métis after the Insurrection," *Saskatchewan
History* 9 (Winter 1956): 3, reports similar values for sale of scrip in
1885 in the North-West Territories.

23.   Sprague, "Manitoba Land Question," 79.

24.   See the introduction to D. N. Sprague and R. P. Frye, "Fur-Trade Company Town: Land and Population in the Red River Settlement 1820-1830," unpublished manuscript. *Métis Land Rights in Alberta*, pp. 146-51, details one case of fraud in northern Alberta. The book, pp. 112-15, explains why the *Métis* sold their scrip, cogently demonstrating that they were not ignorant or childlike in their business dealings; but the authors, inconsistently in my view, still insist on a moralistic denunciation of the speculators.

25.   The petitions are summarized in Stanley, *The Birth of Western Canada*, pp. 246-250.

26.   42 Vict., c.31, s.125(3) (1879). Incorporated with no important change into the Dominion Lands Act of 1883, 46 Vict., c.17, s.81(e).

27.   J. S. Dennis to J. A. Macdonald, 20 December 1878. *CSP* (1885), 1163, 93-96.

28.   "I., Saskatchewan" to J. S. Dennis, 18 January 1879. Ibid., 88-89. (The author is identified as the Anglican Bishop of Saskatchewan in PAC, MG 26 A, 42323.)

29.   A.-A. Taché to J. S. Dennis, 29 January 1879. Ibid., 84-88.

30.   Ibid., 81-83. Other replies were from stipendiary magistrate Hugh Richardson, Lieutenant-Governor David Laird, and the Anglican Bishop of Rupert's Land.

31.   Cited in Stanley, *Birth of Western Canada*, p. 250.

32.   J. A. Macdonald to Lord Lansdowne, 12 August 1887. Joseph Pope, ed., *Correspondence of Sir John Macdonald* (Toronto: Oxford University Press, 1921), p. 318.

33.   *CSP* (1885), 116, 17.

34.   Ibid.

35.   Flanagan, *Louis "David" Riel: "Prophet of the New World,"* p. 132.

36.   Ibid.

37.   Pearce, "All Claims to Land," *CSP* (1886), No. 8b.

38.   H. H. Langton, "The Commission of 1885 to the North-West Territories," *Canadian Historical Review* 25 (March 1944): 46.

39.   *CSP* (1885), 116, 14.

40.   W. P. R. Street to D. L. Macpherson, 5 April 1885. Ibid., 4.

41.   D. L. Macpherson to W. P. R. Street, 6 April 1885. Ibid., 3.

42.   The office consolidation of the Department of the Interior dealing with half-breed land grants cited the order-in-council of 30 March 1885, as the authority for the distribution which took place in 1885-87. There is no reference to the difficulty raised by Street. PAC, RG 15, Vol. 227.

43.   W. P. R. Street to D. L. Macpherson, 6 April 1885. *CSP* (1885), 116, 3.

44.   PAC, RG 15, Vol. 227.

45.   D. J. Hall, "The Half-Breed Claims Commission," *Alberta History* 25 (1977): 1-8.

46.   Langton, "The Commission of 1885," 50.

47.   Giraud, "The Western Métis after the Insurrection," 3.

48.   Clovis Rondeau, *La Montagne de Bois* (Winnipeg, Canadian Publishers Limited, 1970), p. 134.

CHAPTER FOUR

1. Cited in Peter A. Cumming and Neil H. Mickenberg, *Native Rights in Canada* (Toronto: General Publishing, 1972; second edition), p. 138. I have modernized the orthography.
2. Ibid., p. 148.
3. See ibid., pp. 13–50.
4. Louis Riel, [Mémoire sur les troubles du Nord-Ouest], *Le Canadien*, 26 December 1885. Ms. missing.
5. Ibid.
6. Interview with C. B. Pitblado, *Winnipeg Sun*, 3 July 1885.
7. Thomas Flanagan, ed., "Political Theory of the Red River Resistance: The Declaration of December 8, 1869," *Canadian Journal of Political Science* 11 (1978): 154.
8. *Le Canadien*, 26 December 1885; and Petition "To His Excellency [Grover] Cleveland. . .," [August-September 1885], NARS, Despatches from U.S. Consuls in Winnipeg, No. 441.
9. Cited in Stanley, *Birth of Western Canada*, p. 124.
10. Louis Riel, *L'Amnistie* (Montréal: Bureau du "Nouveau Monde," 1874), p. 22.
11. Ibid.
12. Louis Riel to J. W. Taylor, [2–3 August 1885], NARS, Despatches from U.S. Consuls in Winnipeg, 1869–1906, No. 433; [Manifeste à ses concitoyens américains], [August-November 1885], PAC, MG 27 IC4, 2150–56, 2159–60.
13. Desmond Morton, ed., *The Queen v. Louis Riel* (Toronto: University of Toronto Press, 1974), pp. 358–59.
14. Riel, [Manifeste à ses concitoyens américains], 2150–56, 2159–60.
15. I am indebted to the new research on Jackson carried out by Donald B. Smith and Miriam Carey, although my interpretation differs somewhat from theirs. See Smith, "William Henry Jackson: Riel's Secretary," *The Beaver* 311 (Spring 1981): 10–19; *idem*, "Honoré Joseph Jaxon: A Man Who Lived for Others," *Saskatchewan History* 34 (Autumn 1981): 81–101; Carey, "The Role of W. H. Jackson in the North-West Agitation of 1884-85," Honors Thesis, University of Calgary, Political Science, 1980.
16. [Notes for Speech in Prince Albert], [19 July 1885], PAC, RG 13 B2, 2359, 2345.
17. *Prince Albert Times*, 25 July 1884.
18. W. H. Jackson to "Gentlemen," 23 July 1884, PAC, RG 13 B2, 512–17.
19. W. H. Jackson to Louis Riel, 23 July 1884, PAC, RG 13 B2, 503–9.
20. Louis Riel to Joseph Riel and Louis Lavallée, [25?] [July 1884], PAM, MG 3 D1, No. 418.
21. USL, A. S. Morton Mss. Collection, C555/2/13.9v. Typescript, original missing. Several other typed drafts are in the same collection. None is dated, but the contents match the description of the petition given by Jackson in his letter to "Gentlemen," note 18 *supra*.

22.   Ibid., C555/2/13.9q.
23.   Sgt. W. A. Brooks to L. N. F. Crozier, 21 August 1884, PAC, RG 13 B2, 522–23. Typed copy.
24.   James Isbister to Louis Riel, 4 September 1885, PAM, MG 3 D1, No. 412.
25.   A copy of the memorandum in the hand of Louis Schmidt is included in his "Notes: Mouvement des Métis à St-Laurent Sask. TNO en 1884," AASB, T 29799–80. The original has not been found.
26.   Louis Riel to J.-V. Grandin, [7 September 1884], ACAE, Correspondence of Vital Grandin.
27.   Ibid.
28.   Edgar Dewdney to J. A. Macdonald, 19 September 1884, PAC, MG 26 A, 42897–905. The English translations are in ibid., 42935–41.
29.   A.-E. Forget to Edgar Dewdney, 18 September 1884. Ibid., 42921–34.
30.   Gilles Martel, "Le Messianisme de Louis Riel (1844–1885)," Thèse de doctorat, Paris, 1976, p. 393.
31.   Pétition à "votre excellence en conseil," [September 1884], PAC, RG 13 B2, 42–43.
32.   "Les Métis du Nord-Ouest," Montreal Daily Star, 28 November 1885.
33.   Riel's petition requested a total compensation to natives of 37½ cents per acre, slightly more than one-seventh of the current preemption price of $2.00 per acre.
34.   W. H. Jackson, [Note], [September 1884], PAC, RG 13 B2, 159. The date of the meeting is taken from Jackson to J. Isbister, 8 September 1884, PAC, RG 13 B2, 528.
35.   Louis Riel to W. H. Jackson, 22 September 1884. USL, A. S. Morton Mss. Collection, C555/2/13.7d.
36.   Enclosed in Louis Riel to A.-A. Taché, 24 September 1884. AD, W206.M62F, No. 744, p. 7. Microfilm; the original, once at AASB, is now lost.
37.   There are two drafts of a letter from Riel to Scollen, 1 October 1884, PAC, RG 13 B2, 77 and 531–32. The final letter has not been recovered. The letter to Taylor, 1 October 1884, is in DAMMHS, J. W. Taylor Papers. A partial draft, [1 October 1884], is in PAC, RG 13 B2, 74–76.
38.   Petition "To His Excellency the Governor General in Council, etc." [1 October 1884]. DAMMHS, J. W. Taylor Papers.
39.   Louis Riel to J. W. Taylor, 1 October 1884, DAMMHS, J. W. Taylor Papers.
40.   A trip to Battleford is mentioned in Louis Riel to T. E. Jackson, 29 September 1884. USL, A. S. Morton Mss. Collection, C555/2/13.7e.
41.   A.-A. Taché to Louis Riel, 4 October 1884. AASB, T 29742.
42.   Constantine Scollen to Louis Riel, 10 November 1884. PAM, MG 3 D1, No. 415; Dan Maloney to Louis Riel, 17 November 1884, ibid., No. 416.
43.   Petition "To His Excellency the Governor General in Council," [16

December 1884]. PAC, RG 15, Dominion Lands Branch Correspondence, File 83808. Assertions that the petition was signed by Andrew Spence and W. H. Jackson are made by Stanley, *Louis Riel*, p. 291; and Lewis H. Thomas, "Louis Riel's Petition of Rights, 1884," *Saskatchewan History* 23 (1970): 16–26.

44.   W. H. Jackson to J. A. Chapleau, 16 December 1884. PAC, RG 15, Dominion Lands Branch Correspondence, File 83808.

45.   W. H. Jackson to Frank Oliver, 21 January 1885. USL, A. S. Morton Mss. Collection, C555/2/13.9e. Typescript, original not found.

46.   W. H. Jackson to Louis Riel, 18 December 1885. PAM, MG 3 D1, No. 417.

47.   H. J. Morgan to W. H. Jackson, 5 January 1885; memo by William Pearce, n.d.; PAC, RG 15, Dominion Lands Branch Correspondence, File 83808.

48.   W. H. Jackson to Louis Riel, 27 January 1885. PAC, RG 13 B2, 568–79.

49.   Ibid.

50.   W. H. Jackson, "Summary," n.d. USL, A. S. Morton Mss. Collection, C555/2/13.9o. Typescript, original missing.

51.   W. H. Jackson, "Platform," ibid.

52.   W. H. Jackson to "Dear Michel," 6 September 1886. AASB, T 53009-11.

53.   Louis Riel to Romuald Fiset, 16 June 1885. PAC, RG 13 B2, 1036–43.

54.   W. H. Jackson to Louis Riel, 27 January 1885. PAC, RG 13 B2, 568–79.

55.   Louis Schmidt "Notes," AASB T 29811. It was described in very similar terms by Cicely Jackson to A. S. Morton, 25 June 1932; USL, A. S. Morton Mss. Collection, C555/2/13.5. W. H. Jackson obliquely refers to it in his letter to Riel, 27 January 1885; PAC, RG 13 B2, 579. It is also mentioned in Louis Riel to Julie Riel, 9 June 1885; PAM, MG 3 D1, No. 420.

56.   W. H. Jackson to Frank Oliver, 21 January 1885. USL, A. S. Morton Mss. Collection, C555/2/13.9e.

57.   Affidavit of John Slater, 28 July 1885. USL, A. S. Morton Mss. Collection, C555/2/13.9h.

58.   T. E. Jackson, Letter to the Editor, Toronto *Globe*, 2 July 1885.

59.   W. H. Jackson to "My dear Family," 19 September 1885. PAM, Selkirk Asylum Medical Records, MG 3 C20.

60.   Cited in T. E. Jackson to the Toronto *Globe*, 2 July 1885. Original missing.

CHAPTER FIVE

1.   Howard, *Strange Empire*, p. 376; George Woodcock, *Gabriel Dumont* (Edmonton: Hurtig, 1975), pp. 153-54; Adams, *Prison of Grass*, pp. 134-35; Stanley, *Louis Riel*, pp. 295-98; idem, *Birth of Western Canada*,

pp. 311-12; Creighton, *John A. Macdonald: The Old Chieftain*, pp. 413-14.

2. De Trémaudan, *Histoire de la nation métisse*, pp. 418-19.

3. Adams, *Prison of Grass*; W. M. Davidson, *Louis Riel, 1844-1885* (Calgary: Albertan Publishing Co., 1955), p. 149.

4. The lawsuit is well known. The bequest to the convent at St. Hyacinthe is attested by an acknowledgment from Sister Catherine-Aurélie, Superior of the convent, 27 July 1883. PAM, MG 3 D2, Folder 14.

5. Debts totalling $962.00, plus an undetermined amount of interest, are listed in a draft of Riel's will, [6 November 1885]. AASB, T 53013-14. There may well have been others.

6. Desmond Morton, ed., *The Queen v Louis Riel* (Toronto; University of Toronto Press, 1974), pp. 350-71. Hereafter cited as *Q v LR*.

7. Stanley, *Louis Riel*, p. 144.

8. *Q v LR*, p. 369; and D. H. Macdowall to Edgar Dewdney, 24 November 1884; PAC, MG 26 A, 42959.

9. Louis Riel to James Isbister et al., 5 June 1884; PAC, RG 13 B2, 459-60.

10. *Le Manitoba*, 24 July 1884.

11. Louis Riel to Joseph Riel and Louis Lavallée, [25?] [July 1884]; PAM, MG 3 D1, No. 418.

12. J. A. Macdonald to Lord Lansdowne, 5 August 1884; cited in Creighton, *John A. Macdonald*, p. 388.

13. Ibid.

14. Louis Schmidt, "Notes: Mouvement des Métis à St-Laurent Sask. T.N.O. en 1884"; AASB, T 29794. Entry of 6 September 1884.

15. Témoignage de Charles Nolin et Maxime Lépine, Rapport de M. Cloutier, [September-December 1886]; PAA, Oblate Papers, D-IV-116, typescript. Original in AASB. The reminiscences of Napoleon Nault give another version. Cf. de Trémaudan, *Histoire de la nation métisse*, p. 419.

16. A.-E. Forget to Edgar Dewdney, 18 September 1884; PAM, MG 26 A, 42921-34.

17. Edgar Dewdney to J. A. Macdonald, 19 September 1884; PAM, MG 26 A, 42987-905.

18. Flanagan, ed., *The Diaries of Louis Riel*, p. 47.

19. Nolin and Lépine: statement in report of Father Cloutier, PAA, Oblate Papers, D-IV-116. Cf. note 15.
   Nolin (I): testimony in *Q v LR*, pp. 194-96.
   Nolin (II): statement of evidence, PAC, RG 13 B2, 3219-23.
   Nolin (III): statement in report of Father Cloutier, as cited in Martel, "Le Messianisme de Louis Riel," pp. 428-30.
   André (I): testimony in *Q v LR*, pp. 233-34.
   André (II): letter to Father Coffey, editor of the *Catholic Record* (London), n.d. but *ca.* July 1885. AD, microfilm 720, pp. 1-30. Original once at AASB, now lost.
   André (III): letter to Edgar Dewdney, [December 1884], PAC, MG 27

IC4, 24-27; clerk's copy, PAC, MG 26 A, 42954-57.
André (IV): letter to Edgar Dewdney, 21 January 1885; PAC, MG 27
IC4, 28-30; clerk's copy, PAC, MG 26 A, 42971-73.
André (V): letter to Edgar Dewdney, 6 February 1885; PAC, MG 27
IC4, 32-35; Eng. trans., PAC, MG 26 A, 42995-99.
Schmidt: "Notes"; cf. note 14 *supra*.
Macdowall (I): letter to Edgar Dewdney, 24 December 1884; PAC, MG
26 A, 42958-60; clerk's copy, PAC, MG 27 IC4, 1329-34.
Macdowall (II): letter to Edgar Dewdney, 14 January 1885; GAI,
Dewdney Papers, 1406-9.
Macdowall (III): telegram to Edgar Dewdney, 3 February 1885; PAC,
MG 27 IC4, 1337.

20. Nolin and Lépine.
21. Nolin (I), 194.
22. André (II).
23. Schmidt.
24. André (II).
25. Macdowall (I).
26. André (III).
27. Joseph Howe to L. N. F. Crozier, 24 December 1884; PAC, MG 26 A, 42304 (typed copy).
28. Nolin (I), 195.
29. Nolin (III), 428. Confirmed also in Nolin (II), 3221.
30. Thomas Flanagan, "The Riel 'Lunacy Commission': The Report of Dr. Valade," *Revue de l'Université d'Ottawa* 46 (1976): 121.
31. Speech of Charles Fitzpatrick, *Q v LR*, pp. 301-2.
32. Speech of Christopher Robinson, *Q v LR*, pp. 330-31.
33. André (II).
34. *Le Manitoba*, 12 February 1885.
35. Schmidt, 29810.
36. L. N. F. Crozier to Edgar Dewdney, 7 January 1885; PAC, MG 26 A, 42302-03.
37. Schmidt, 29811.
38. Macdowall (II).
39. André (IV).
40. Nolin (I), 196.
41. The account is basically the same in Nolin (I), (II), and (III).
42. *Q v LR*, pp. 316-17.
43. Nolin (II), 3223.
44. André (V); Macdowall (III).
45. L. N. F. Crozier to Edgar Dewdney, 2 and 3 February 1885; PAC, MG 26 A, 42975.
46. André (V).
47. J. A. Macdonald to Edgar Dewdney, 20 February 1885; GAI, Dewdney Papers, 545 ff.
48. *Diaries of Louis Riel*, p. 78.

CHAPTER SIX

1. PAC, RG 13 A 2, Vol. 62, file 596. C. Robinson and B. B. Osler to the Minister of Justice, 16 June 1885.
2. De Trémaudan, *Histoire de la nation métisse*, pp. 344-45.
3. Howard, *Strange Empire*, p. 508.
4. L. H. Thomas, "A Judicial Murder — The Trial of Louis Riel," in Howard Palmer, ed., *The Settlement of the West* (Calgary: Comprint Publishing, 1977), p. 59.
5. *Louis Riel: Justice Must Be Done* (Winnipeg: Manitoba Métis Federation Press, 1979), p. 85.
6. Morton, *Q v LR*, p. xxix.
7. F. A. Hayek, *Law, Legislation and Liberty* (Chicago: The University of Chicago Press, 1973-79), *passim*.
8. Sandra Bingaman, "The Trials of the 'White Rebels,' 1885," *Saskatchewan History* 25 (1972): 45. See also her "The Trials of Poundmaker and Big Bear, 1885," ibid 28 (1975): 81-94; and "The North West Rebellion Trials, 1885," M.A. Thesis, University of Saskatchewan at Regina, 1971.
9. D. H. Brown, "The Meaning of Treason in 1885," *Saskatchewan History* 28 (1975): 65-73.
10. R. E. Turner, "The Life and Death of Louis Riel: Part III — Medico-Legal Issues," *Canadian Psychiatric Association Journal* 10 (1965): 259-63.
11. Thomas, "A Judicial Murder."
12. Morton, "Introduction," *Q v LR*.
13. Ibid., p. xv.
14. Thomas Flanagan and Neil Watson, "The Riel Trial Revisited," *Saskatchewan History* 34 (1981): 57-73. The present chapter is largely based on this article.
15. Of course, such comparisons cannot be pushed too far because treasonous episodes in the nineteenth century were widely spaced and quite different in their circumstances.
16. Morton, *Q v LR*, p. xxiii.
17. Mr. Justice Riddell, "Canadian State Trials: The King v David McLane," *Transactions of the Royal Society of Canada* 16 (1916): 332-34.
18. See Flanagan and Watson, "The Riel Trial Revisited," 73, note 20.
19. Ibid., note 21.
20. Ibid., note 22.
21. See the Appendix in ibid., 70-71.
22. Ibid., 73, note 23.
23. See Thomas, "A Judicial Murder," 38-39.
24. *CSP*, 1886, Paper No. 52, p. 174.
25. 31 Vict., c.69, s.5 (1868).
26. Ibid., s.8. Curiously, in spite of this statutory provision, Macdonald himself felt that there might have been some difficulty in applying treason-felony to Riel's case. See. P. B. Waite, *Canada 1874-1896: Arduous Destiny* (Toronto, 1970), p. 162.

27.   It would appear that it was for just that reason — to have available a more moderate alternative at the discretion of the Crown — that the provision of treason-felony was first introduced in 1848. A report of the first treason-felony trial, the Queen v. John Mitchel (See *State Trials*, new series, Vol. VI, p. 600) suggests that the need for such a provision was precipitated by the undesirable prospect of constantly facing High Treason's severe punishment when dealing with the persistent Fenian activities.

28.   36 Vict., c.34, schedule A (1873).

29.   11 and 12 Vict., c.12 (1848).

30.   See for example Rex. v McCafferty, *Cox's Criminal Cases*, Vol. LX, p. 603. Unfortunately, no late nineteenth-century series of trials resulting from one rebellion could be uncovered in which charges of both treason and treason-felony were laid to make any comparisons with the North-West Rebellion trials in the indicting of principals and lesser figures.

31.   Cf. Bingaman's thesis, cit. note 8.

32.   PAC, R.G. 13 B 2, 1034. Louis Riel to Charles Fitzpatrick and F.-X. Lemieux, 18 June 1885.

33.   Ibid., 1074-77 and 1151-54. 24 and 27 June 1885.

34.   Desmond Morton and R. H. Roy, *Telegrams of the North-West Campaign* (Toronto: Champlain Society, 1972), pp. 288, 302, 308.

35.   Morton, *Q v LR*, p. viii; Thomas, "A Judicial Murder," 39.

36.   36 Vict., c.35, s.5 (1873); 38 Vict., c.49, s.66 (1875).

37.   43 Vict., c.45, s.71-84 (1880).

38.   See 40 Vict., c.7 (1877).

39.   The following letters will be found in Public Archives of Canada MG 26 A, (Macdonald Papers):

    82791-94   -   13 April 1885
    82799   -   16 April 1885
    82813-15   -   18 May 1885
    82817   -   20 May 1885
    82819-23   -   21 May 1885
    82862-67   -   17 June 1885

40.   PAC, MG 26A, 82819-23, 21 May 1885.

41.   Turner, "The Life and Death of Louis Riel," 260.

42.   Ibid.

43.   Thomas, "A Judicial Murder," p. 48.

44.   See 48 Vict., C.45 (1880).

45.   The trial transcript is in *CSP*, 52 (1886), 340-344. For other analyses of Jackson's trial see Sandra Bingaman, "The Trials of the 'White Rebels,' 1885" and Cyril Greenland and John Griffin, "William Henry Jackson (1861-1952): Riel's Secretary: Another Case of Involuntary Confinement,"*Canadian Psychiatric Association Journal* 23 (1978): 469-77.

46.   43 Vict., c.25, s.9 (1880).

47.   The jury list was printed in *Epitome of Parliamentary Documents in Connection with the North-West Rebellion 1885* (Ottawa: MacLean, Roger and Co., 1886), p. 13.

48.   Montreal *Daily Star*, 29 July 1885.
49.   *Q v LR*, p. 15.
50.   1st and 2nd George IV, c.66 (1821).
51.   22 and 23 Vict., c.26, s.1 (1859).
52.   28 and 29 Vict., c.63 (1865).
53.   *Q v LR*, p. 28.
54.   Queen v. Goodhue, 19 Grant (1872).
55.   *Q v LR*, p. 30.
56.   Queen v. Connor, *Territories Law Reports*, 4 (29 June 1885).
57.   *Q v LR*, p. 36.
58.   Queen v. Riel, 2 *Manitoba Law Reports*, 321, at 351 (9 September 1885).
59.   John Biggs, *The Guilty Mind* (Baltimore: Johns Hopkins Press, 1955), ch. 4.
60.   Simon N. Verdun-Jones, " 'Not Guilty by Reason of Insanity': The Historical Roots of the Canadian Insanity Defence, 1843-1920," in Louis A. Knalfla, ed., *Crime and Criminal Justice in Europe and Canada* (Waterloo, Ont.: Wilfrid Laurier University Press, 1981), p. 183.
61.   Cited in H. Barnes, "A Century of the McNaghten Rules," *Cambridge Law Journal* 8 (1944): 300.
62.   Roger Smith, *Trial by Medicine: Insanity and Responsibility in Victorian Trials* (Edinburgh: Edinburgh University Press, 1981).
63.   *Q v LR*, p. 348.
64.   Verdun-Jones, " 'Not Guilty by Reason of Insanity'," p. 193.
65.   *Q v LR*, p. 257.
66.   Ibid., p. 260.
67.   Ibid., p. 296.
68.   Queen v. Riel, 2 *Manitoba Law Reports*, 321, at 329.
69.   Ibid., p. 344.
70.   Ibid., p. 345.
71.   Criminal Code (1892), s.11(1), in Verdun-Jones, " 'Not Guilty by Reason of Insanity'," p. 197.

CHAPTER SEVEN

1.   *House of Commons Debates*, 1885, p. 693.
2.   Ibid., p. 764.
3.   Ibid., p. 3117.
4.   The daughter of the foreman Francis Cosgrave said in 1955, "Father knew Riel was innocent," Toronto *Globe and Mail*, 22 July 1955. However, this is so far after the event as not to be a reliable statement. Another juror wrote to Edward Blake: "We could not but condemn in the strongest terms possible the extraordinary dilatoriness of Sir John Macdonald, Sir David McPherson, and Lieutenant Governor Dewdney," *House of Commons Debates*, 1886, 255. A third said forty years later: "We often remarked during the trial that we would like to have the Minister of the Interior in the prisoner's box," W. M. Davidson,

The Life and Times of Louis Riel (Calgary: Albertan Printers, 1951), p. 104.

5. The petition, dated 28 October 1885, is printed as an annex to *The Queen vs Louis Riel* (Ottawa: Queen's Printer, 1886), pp. 204-205.
6. Roger Smith, *Trial by Medicine: Insanity and Responsibility in Victorian Trials,* (Edinburgh: Edinburgh University Press, 1981).
7. PAC, MG 26 A, 42612 ff.
8. E.C.B., "The Mission of Dr. Lavell," *Douglas Library Notes* 12 (1963):9.
9. A longer discussion of Dr. Valade will be found in Thomas Flanagan, "The Riel 'Lunacy Commission': The Report of Dr. Valade," *Revue de l'Université d'Ottawa* 46 (1976): 108-27. This chapter is a modified version of that article.
10. Macdonald to Lavell, 31 October 1885. Published in *Douglas Library Notes* 12 (1963): 17.
11. Stanley, *Louis Riel,* p. 366.
12. Jukes to Macdonald, 6 November 1885; PAC, MG 26 A, 42632-33.
13. Dewdney to Macdonald, 7 November 1885; ibid., 42644.
14. Jukes to Macdonald, 9 November 1885; ibid., 42652-78.
15. Lavell to Macdonald, 9 November 1885; ibid., 42672-74.
16. Ibid., 42648.
17. Valade to Macdonald, 9 November 1885; ibid., 42650-51.
18. Dewdney to Macdonald, 9 November 1885; ibid., 42645-46.
19. Lavell to Macdonald, 9 November 1885; ibid., 42685.
20. PAC, MG 26 A, 42963-42700.
21. *Le Canada* (Ottawa), 20 November 1885.
22. Archives of Ontario, Edward Blake Papers, Microfilm in PAC, reel M246. Sir Wilfrid Laurier also knew something was up. On 31 December 1885 he wrote to Blake: "As to the reports of the confidential commissioners, it is said that Lavell had reported monomania, and Valade complete insanity. I understand this to come from Forget." Ibid., M240.
23. *CSP* (1886), no. 43.
24. Creighton, *John A. Macdonald: The Old Chieftain,* p. 447.
25. PAC, Caron Papers, Lavell to Caron, 14 December 1885. Vol. 193, p. 005419.
26. Ibid., Vol. 193, pp. 005386-96.
27. *House of Commons Debates,* 15 March 1886, p. 122.
28. After this episode Valade had two private audiences with Sir John, 6 November 1888 and 15 December 1890. These are attested in the Macdonald Papers, 231718-9 and 245990-1; but no record exists of what was discussed.
29. Dr. F.-X. Valade, Report on the Mental Condition of Louis Riel, 1885, MG 27 I J 8.
30. Smith, *Trial by Medicine,* p. 37.
31. Flanagan, "The Riel 'Lunacy Commission'," 127.
32. Ibid.
33. H. Barnes, "A Century of the McNaghten Rules," *Cambridge Law Journal* 8 (1944): 319.

CHAPTER EIGHT

1. Association of Métis and Non-Status Indians of Saskatchewan, *Louis Riel: Justice Must Be Done* (Winnipeg: Manitoba Métis Federation Press, 1979), pp. 85-86.

2. For a survey see Leslie Sebba, " 'The Pardoning Power — A World Survey'," *The Journal of Criminal Law and Criminology* 68 (1977): 83-121.

3. R.S.C. 1970, c.34, s.683. The Criminal Records Act (S.C., 1969-70, c.40) created still another type of pardon awarded upon a period of good conduct after release from prison. The major purpose of this provision is to wipe out the criminal records of those who seem rehabilitated. Of 7566 applications in 1978-79 fiscal year, 3808 were granted by the governor general in council upon recommendation of the National Parole Board transmitted by the solicitor general. This type of pardon has no bearing on Riel's case.

4. R.S.C. 1970, c.34, s.686.

5. Annual Report of the Solicitor General for 1978-79.

6. C. H. Rolph, *The Queen's Pardon* (London: Cassell, 1978), p. 87.

7. Letter to the author from Hélène Chevalier, Chief of the Clemency and Criminal Records Division, National Parole Board, 26 November 1981.

8. *Ex parte* Garland, 4 Wall. 333, at 380 (1866), cited in Samuel Williston, "Does a Pardon Blot Out Guilt?" *Harvard Law Review* 28 (1915): 647.

9. *Report of a Committee Appointed to Inquire into the Principles and Procedures Followed in the Remission Service of the Department of Justice of Canada* (Fauteux Report), (Ottawa: Queen's Printer, 1956), p. 33.

10. Ibid., p. 34.

11. *Q v LR*, p. 350.

12. Cited in the introduction by J. G. Randall to Jonathan Truman Dorris, *Pardon and Amnesty under Lincoln and Johnson* (Chapel Hill: University of North Carolina Press, 1953), pp. xiii–xiv.

13. For a historical survey of cases of amnesty and pardon, see George C. Killinger et. al., *Probation and Parole in the Criminal Justice System* (St. Paul, Minn.: West Publishing Co., 1976), pp. 326-36.

14. Mason Wade, *The French Canadians 1760-1967* (Toronto: Macmillan of Canada, 1968; rev. ed.), p. 194. The four were L.-H. Lafontaine, A.-N. Morin, G.-E. Cartier, E.-P. Taché.

ABBREVIATIONS

PUBLICATIONS

CSP	*Canadian Sessional Papers*
Q v LR	Desmond Morton, ed., *The Queen v Louis Riel* (Toronto: University of Toronto Press, 1974)
R.S.C.	Revised Statutes of Canada
S.M.	Statutes of Manitoba
S.C.	Statutes of Canada

MANUSCRIPT COLLECTIONS CONSULTED

Abbre-viation	Archive	Collection Code (if any)	Name of collection
AASB	Archives de l'Archevêché de Saint-Boniface	T	Fonds Taché
ACAE	Archives of the Catholic Archdiocese of Edmonton		Correspondence of Vital Grandin
AD	Archives Deschâtelets (Ottawa)	W206 M62F	Microfilms des AASB
DAMMHS	Division of Archives and Manuscripts, Minnesota Historical Society		James Wickes Taylor Papers

GAI	Glenbow-Alberta Institute		Edgar Dewdney Papers
PAA	Prov. Archives of Alberta		Oblate Papers
PAC	Public Archives of Canada	MG 26 A	John A. Macdonald Papers
PAC	Public Archives of Canada	MG 27 I C 4	Edgar Dewdney Papers
PAC	Public Archives of Canada	MG 27 I D 3	Adolphe Caron Papers
PAC	Public Archives of Canada	MG 27 I J 8	F.-X. Valade Papers
PAC	Public Archives of Canada	RG 10	Indian Affairs
PAC	Public Archives of Canada	RG 13 A 2	Department of Justice
PAC	Public Archives of Canada	RG 13 B 2	Department of Justice
PAC	Public Archives of Canada	RG 15	Department of the Interior
PAM	Prov. Archives of Manitoba	MG 3 C 20	Selkirk Asylum Medical Records
PAM	Prov. Archives of Manitoba	MG 3 D 1	Louis Riel Collection
PAM	Prov. Archives of Manitoba	MG 3 D 2	Riel Family Papers
SAB (S)	Saskatchewan Archives Board (Saskatoon)		Homestead Files
SAB (S)	Saskatchewan Archives Board (Saskatoon)	AG 11	Department of Agriculture, Lands Branch
UAA	University of Alberta Archives		William Pearce Papers
USL	University of Saskatchewan Libraries		A. S. Morton Manuscript Collection

INDEX